The Italian Family Cookbook

Great Italian Recipes for Families Everywhere

by
Alessandra Russolillo-Schneider
Lisa Russolillo

Cookbook Resources, LLC

i

The Italian Family Cookbook

Great Italian Recipes for Families Everywhere

1st Printing March 2006

ISBN 1-931294-92-5
Library of Congress Number: 2006920300

Illustrated by Nancy Griffith
Edited, Designed and Published in the
United States of America
Manufactured in China
by
Cookbook Resources, LLC
541 Doubletree Drive
Highland Village, Texas 75077
Toll free 866-229-2665
www.cookbookresources.com

cookbook resources® LLC
Bringing Families To The Table

The Authentic Italian Experience

"For our children, we have created *The Italian Family Cookbook*. We want our children to preserve and to protect our family's authentic Italian recipes. And, we want our children to pass on to their children that the essence of the Italian family experience is sharing the food with family and friends."

Anyone who has spent a significant amount of time in Italy will probably tell you that food is the focal point of Italian life. It is the sharing of food and gathering with family and friends that is the true Italian way.

Since we no longer live in Italy, we try to create some of the vivacious lifestyle through the only means we know: authentic Italian family cooking. Many of the meals we have captured in this cookbook have been served in our families for generations without written recipes.

Using recipes handed down from one mamma to the next or, in many cases, from one papa to the next, we create meals that represent the authentic Italian experience. Such meals do not require enormous amounts of effort and time. They only require that your heart be in it.

A few traditional Italian ingredients are also necessary, but personal preferences are too. Making a dish yours by adding a little more crushed red pepper or a little less parsley is very much a part of the Italian experience.

Meals are never just about eating. They are about the whole ritual that precedes the actual meal and are as much a part of the experience as the meal itself. We truly believe that our moods affect the outcome of the food. We believe that proper preparation is fundamental and that the inviting presentation of the food is essential. In Italy we say, "Anche l'occhio vuole la sua parte" or "The eye wants its part".

Meals are events. They are not about survival, but they are about nourishment for the mind, body and soul. An Italian meal involves a carefully orchestrated symphony of tastes and textures and it should be shared with family and friends. Somehow, taking even the most insignificant meal seriously creates the opportunity for one of life's greatest pleasures and best memories.

We hope that our family recipes can bring as much joy to your table as they bring to ours. And, through this cookbook, you can feel the strength and wisdom of sharing meals with family and friends.

About Italy...

The Food of Central Italy

There are five distinct regions in central Italy and the Russolillo family comes from the region of Lazio and the city of Rome. Here Italian food is mostly classical, yet there is a sensible and practical approach to cooking.

Cooking from this central region of Italy and specifically Rome still reflects many of the traditions and characteristics of early Roman cooking. People shop in open-air markets for the freshest fruits and vegetables and seasonal foods are served when they are the best.

Other central regions surrounding Rome include Tuscany, Emilia-Romagna, Umbria and the Marche. Tuscany is world famous for its food and is the model of culinary perfection. Its cuisine is not filled with rich creamy sauces, but rather the natural flavors of Tuscan meats and vegetables adorned only by the extra virgin olive oil made around Florence, Siena and Lucca.

Most notable culinary delights from Tuscany include the purest, extra virgin olive oils and chianti wine. Most notable delights from Emilia-Romagna include parmigiano reggiano, prosciutto, parma ham, sausages and egg pasta. Most notable from Umbria are olives and black truffles. Most notable from the Marche are fried olives and verdicchio, one of Italy's best white wines as well as numerous fish dishes.

The Meal

The authentic Italian meal is an event with different courses all designed to blend flavors and textures for the best experience. **Antipasti** is a beginning of the meal. Its purpose is to entice each person's taste buds. The one consistent ingredient for all antipasti, just as it is in all Italian cooking, is olive oil. The distinctive taste is a must to get the senses of taste ready for what's to come. Also, essential to the beginning of the meal is for the antipasti to look beautiful enough to arouse the imagination.

The first course, **I Primi**, usually includes pasta, the mainstay and trademark of Italian cooking. In most regions of Italy pasta is a mixture of flour, water, salt and eggs. It has become one of the most popular and most recognized Italian dishes. Soups, stews, risottas and stuffings may also be included in the first course.

I Secondi or second course is the considered the main course of the meal and usually features beef, chicken, pork or game. Fish is sometimes used, as are egg dishes prepared in a variety of ways.

Verdure E Contorni, vegetables and side dishes, or **Stuzzichini**, fun side dishes usually follow the main course. This course consists of vegetables cooked in a variety of ways all designed to lock in the fresh flavors of the produce.

I Dolci is the last course and includes sweet cakes, pastries, fruits, fritters and desserts. Most are not ornate or difficult, but simple and not-too-sweet.

The Pasta

As the most recognized Italian food, pasta in Italy dates back before Marco Polo returned from China bringing noodles in 1295. The Italians have been making pasta and creating dishes that are known around the world.

The best variety of wheat for making pasta is durum or grano duro. The flour from durum wheat is called semola in Italian. For the best quality pasta, look for these words on the package: *pasta di semola di grano duro*. It may be a little more expensive, but it won't stick together like pasta made with a softer wheat. Generally, the Italian brands are best.

The main ingredients used with Italian pasta dishes include extra virgin olive oil, fresh or canned tomatoes, olives, garlic, red bell peppers, onions and parsley.

Italians do not regard dried pasta as inferior to fresh homemade pasta. It is just a different form of pasta and is extremely popular world-wide.

Pasta is an extremely nutritional food containing as much protein as steak but with little or no fat. It is rich in protein, vitamins and minerals and is a complex carbohydrate food. Because pasta contains six of the eight amino acids needed for protein, it only needs a few ingredients to make it complete.

Italians keep pasta simple and use small amounts of cheese, meat, fish, vegetables, eggs and/or extra virgin olive oil. By adding small amounts of sauces and other foods, Italian pasta dishes are extremely well balanced and nutritional.

Italians have one of the lowest percentages of heart disease of any nation in the world. Because pasta makes up such a large portion of their diet, scientists believe pasta and what Italians put with pasta accounts for the low occurrence of heart disease.

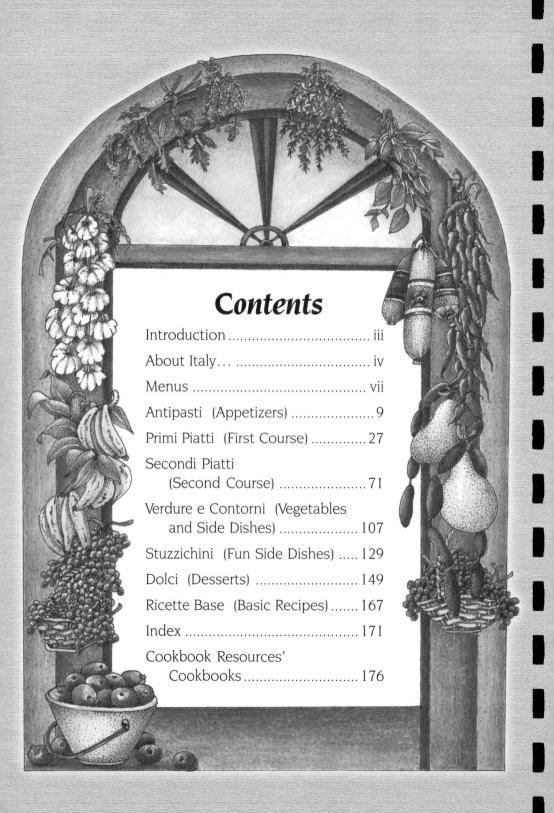

Contents

Menus For Family and Friends

Menus For Family and Friends

Antipasti
Appetizers

— per iniziare stuzzicando —

— We begin by munching. —

Affettato Misto
(Italian Cold Cuts and Cheese Platter)

These classic Italian meats and cheeses served with fresh crusty bread make a delicious start to a meal or just a snack.

10 very thin slices prosciutto crudo
10 thin slices mortadella
10 thin slices salame, Genoa or hard
Provolone, cubed
Parmigiano, cubed
Fontina, cubed
Assorted olives
Cherry tomatoes

- On large platter, arrange all cold cuts around outside of platter.
- Place cheese cubes in center.
- Garnish with green olives, black olives and cherry tomatoes.

Serves 6.

Antipasto is the beginning of the meal. Its purpose is to get the taste buds working and ready for the courses to follow.

Caprese
(Mozzarella Cheese with Roma Tomatoes and Fresh Basil)

This is a very popular dish especially in the hot summer months.

4 Roma tomatoes
8 slices fresh mozzarella cheese
3 tablespoons extra-virgin olive oil   **45 ml**
8-10 leaves fresh basil

- Slice tomatoes and mozzarella into ½-inch (1.2 cm) thick, round pieces.
- Arrange tomatoes and mozzarella slices in overlapping, alternating pattern on serving dish.
- Drizzle olive oil over arrangement and sprinkle with salt and pepper to taste.
- Place fresh basil leaves on top of mozzarella slices.

Serves 4.

Pinzimonio
(Vegetable Dip)

A bold, robust olive oil is perfect for this very easy starter. It's really the key to this wonderful appetizer.

10 baby carrots	
4 celery stalks, cut lengthwise	
1 cucumber	
1 red bell pepper	
1 cup mayonnaise	**240 ml**
4 tablespoons whipping cream	**60 ml**
1 tablespoon spicy mustard	**15 ml**
1 tablespoon chives	**15 ml**

- Wash and slice all vegetables.
- In separate bowl, combine mayonnaise, cream and mustard. Stir to mix well and mixture is smooth. Add a little pepper and chopped chives.
- Arrange vegetables on serving platter. Place bowl full of vegetable dip in center. Enjoy.

Serves 4.

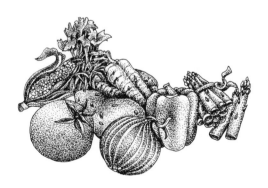

Bruschetta con Pomodoro
(Toasted Italian Bread with Tomatoes)

Bruschetta is as Italian as it gets. The crusty bread with fresh tomatoes and fresh herbs make this everyone's favorite.

8-10 slices toasted Italian bread
2 fresh garlic cloves, peeled
4 Roma tomatoes, chopped
4-5 tablespoons extra-virgin olive oil   **60-75 ml**
8-10 fresh basil leaves

- Preheat oven to 400° (204°).
- Cut bread into ½-inch (1.2 cm) slices and put on baking sheet. Place in oven to toast.
- Rub garlic cloves on toasted bread slices.
- In small bowl, add chopped tomatoes, olive oil, basil and salt and pepper to taste. Stir to mix well.
- Place about 1 tablespoon (15 ml) tomato mixture on each bread slice. Enjoy!

Serves 6.

Garlic was considered a sacred herb of the Ancient Egyptians. Greek Olympian athletes used to chew garlic. And, even today it is considered good for healthy hearts. We love the wonderful things fresh garlic can do to liven up a dish. It's bold, yet sweet flavor is essential in so many of our recipes. We always recommend using fresh garlic, but if that's not possible, the jar of minced garlic will do just fine. When shopping for fresh garlic, remember to select bulbs that are firm, with no sprouts.

Bruschetta con Aglio e Olio
(Toasted Italian Bread with Garlic and Olive Oil)

Originally bruschetta was created to use old or stale bread. Brushing the best olive oil over the bread and seasoning it with fresh garlic makes this bread fit for a king.

8-10 slices toasted Italian bread
2 fresh garlic cloves, peeled
Olive oil

- Preheat oven to 400° (204°).
- Cut bread into ½-inch (1.2 cm) slices and place on baking sheet. Put bread in oven to toast.
- Rub garlic cloves on toasted bread slices.
- Brush desired amount of olive oil on each slice of bread.
- Add salt and pepper to taste.

Serves 6.

Olive oil is the Mediterranean's "liquid gold" and is used for all Italian cooking. The two most common varieties of olive are extra virgin or "light" and olive oil or "dark." Extra virgin olive oil is better suited for salads and marinades rather than cooking. It is purely a matter of preference as to which kind you prefer. However, whether your choice is "dark" or "light", you should always keep a bottle in your pantry. There is no Italian cooking without olive oil.

Crostini Ai Funghi
(Mushroom Crostini)

Crostini are little pieces of toasted bread. Any topping is excellent on it, but we think mushrooms, cheese and pate are the best toppings.

6 ounces porcini mushrooms	**168 g**
4 tablespoons olive oil	**60 ml**
1 clove garlic, peeled, crushed	
2 tablespoons finely chopped parsley	**30 ml**
1 tablespoon flour	**15 ml**
4 slices rustic Italian bread	

- Preheat oven to 400° (204°).
- Wash mushrooms, remove stems and slice.
- Combine oil, garlic and parsley in skillet over medium heat. Add mushrooms, salt and pepper to taste. Cook for about 10 minutes.
- Add flour and continuously stir flour and mushrooms for about 5 more minutes. Remove from heat, cover and set aside.
- Place bread slices on baking sheet and place in oven to toast. Place mushroom mixture on each bread slice and serve.

Serves 4.

Prosciutto Crudo con Fichi
(Prosciutto Ham with Figs)

Prosciutto is thinly sliced ham from the Parma and San Daniele regions of Italy and is considered a delicacy.

10 very thin slices prosciutto crudo
6 ripe green or black figs, sliced into wedges
Rustic Italian bread, sliced

- Arrange slices of prosciutto crudo on serving plate.
- Peel figs and slice into 4 wedges.
- Place figs on top of prosciutto crudo. Serve with sliced, crusty Italian bread.

Serves 4.

Prosciutto Crudo con Melone
(Prosciutto Ham with Cantaloupe)

Different fruits and vegetables are wonderful served with prosciutto and cantaloupe is a great choice.

10 very thin slices prosciutto crudo
1 ripe cantaloupe

- Peel cantaloupe and slice into wedges.
- Wrap prosciutto slices around cantaloupe wedges.
- Arrange wedges of prosciutto-wrapped cantaloupe around perimeter of serving platter. Serve chilled.

Serves 4.

Antipasto Vegetale
(Mixed Grilled Vegetable Platter)

Even the pickiest eaters will love these simple vegetables served with fresh bread or crackers.

1 eggplant, thinly sliced	
2 zucchini, thinly sliced	
1 red pepper, thinly sliced	
1 green pepper, thinly sliced	
1 yellow pepper, thinly sliced	
2 large tomatoes, thickly sliced	
⅓ cup olive oil	**80 ml**
2 teaspoons minced garlic	**10 ml**
¼ cup finely chopped parsley, divided	**60 ml**

- Preheat oven for grilling or prepare outdoor grill.
- Grill vegetables until tender, but firm.
- In small bowl, add olive oil, garlic, half the chopped parsley, salt and pepper. Mix well.
- Brush mixture on freshly grilled vegetables.
- Garnish with remaining parsley. Serve warm.

Serves 4 to 6.

Insalata di Mare
(Mixed Fresh Seafood Salad)

This is a popular dish all over Italy, especially along the beautiful blue coasts of the "boot".

1 rib celery	
5 baby carrots, sliced	
6 ounces squid rounds	**168 g**
6 ounces shrimp, peeled, veined	**168 g**
1 pound fresh mussels	**.5 kg**
1 pound fresh clams	**.5 kg**
1 garlic clove, peeled, finely chopped	
¼ cup white wine	**60 ml**
4 tablespoons extra-virgin olive oil	**60 ml**
2 tablespoons fresh lemon juice	**30 ml**
¼ cup chopped parsley	**60 ml**
5 leaves fresh basil, chopped	

- Bring large pot of water to boil. Add ribs from celery stalk, carrots and squid. Cook squid for approximately 10 minutes. Remove squid and set aside.

- Add shrimp and continue to cook in pot for about 2 to 3 minutes or until shrimp turn pink. Remove shrimp, carrots and celery. Chop carrots and celery and set aside.

- In separate saucepan, combine mussels, clams, pinch of chopped garlic and white wine. Cover and steam until shells open. Remove mussels and clams from shells.

- In large serving bowl, combine all seafood, chopped celery and carrots. Add olive oil, remainder of chopped garlic, lemon juice, parsley, basil, salt and pepper to taste. Stir to mix well. Chill before serving.

Serves 6.

Tip: Fresh seafood is always the best, but frozen works very well.

Il Cocktail di Gamberetti
(Shrimp Cocktail)

This is a perfect way to begin a wonderful dinner with fish entrees.

½ **tablespoon rock salt**	**7 ml**
½ **pound small frozen shrimp, peeled, veined**	**227 g**
4 large leaves Boston lettuce	
5 tablespoons olive oil, divided	**75 ml**
Juice of 1 lemon, seeds removed	

- Fill pot with water and rock salt and bring to boil. Cook shrimp in boiling water for 3 minutes. Drain and place in bowl. Add 2½ tablespoons (37 ml) olive oil. Stir to mix well and set aside.
- In separate bowl, combine lemon juice, remaining olive oil, salt and pepper to taste. Whisk with fork to mix well.
- In individual serving cups, place leaf of lettuce and several scoops of shrimp. Drizzle olive oil and lemon juice mixture over shrimp. Chill and serve.

Serves 4.

Salt is fundamental to good cooking. The type of salt we commonly use is **rock salt**. It is an essential part of cooking pasta. We typically add it to boiling water prior to cooking the pasta. Just a small amount will boost the flavor of the final dish.

Il Cocktail di Gamberetti Rustico

(Rustic Shrimp Cocktail)

This hearty shrimp dish may be served as an appetizer or an entrée with fresh bread.

½ **tablespoon rock salt**	**7 ml**
½ **pound small frozen shrimp, peeled, veined**	**227 g**
1 (15 ounce) can cannellini beans, drained	**425 g**
3 tablespoons olive oil	**45 ml**
1 tablespoon balsamic vinegar	**15 ml**
4 leaves fresh basil, crushed	

- Fill pot with water and rock salt and bring to boil. Cook shrimp in boiling water for 3 minutes. Drain and place in bowl. Add beans, olive oil, vinegar, basil, salt and pepper to taste. Stir to mix well.
- In individual serving cups, place leaf of lettuce and several scoops of shrimp mixture. Chill and serve.

Serves 4.

Antipasto di Salmone
(Salmon Platter)

This simple, elegant dish is a guaranteed hit for any dinner party or casual get-together.

1 (8 ounce) package salmon	227 g
2 eggs, hard-boiled	
½ cup red onion, chopped	120 ml
3 tablespoons capers	45 ml
1 (4 ounce) package cream cheese	114 g
Crackers	

- Arrange salmon slices on large serving platter.
- Peel and dice hard-boiled eggs and place in middle of platter.
- Place capers and chopped onions in middle next to eggs.
- Place cream cheese and crackers on separate plate. Enjoy!

Serves 4 to 6.

Capperi (Capers)- Capers are actually flower buds from a bush found in many Mediterranean countries. The buds are dried, then pickled in vinegar with salt. If you find the taste of capers to be too salty, you may want to rinse them first before adding them to your recipe.

Prosciutto Cotto con Bocconcini
(Ham with Fresh Mozzarella)

These delectable morsels are so much better than chips and dips and everyone enjoys them.

6-8 slices prosciutto cotto, cut into strips
2 containers fresh buffalo mozzarella, cubed
Cherry tomatoes

- Cut ham into ½ inch to 1-inch (2.5 cm) strips. Cut mozzarella into bite-size pieces.
- Wrap ham around each mozzarella piece (bocconcini) and secure with toothpick.
- Arrange ham and bocconcini on plate and garnish with cherry tomatoes.
- Serve chilled.

Serves 4 to 6.

Prosciutto is the Italian word for ham. Prosciutto cotto refers to cooked ham.

Bocconcini is the Italian word for "mouthful" and refers to bite-size pieces of mozzarella, but is sometimes applied to other foods as well.

Tartine Tonno e Pomodoro
(Tuna and Tomato Tartlets)

Many Italian recipes use tomatoes prepared in a variety of ways. This outstanding appetizer combines the flavor of tomatoes with other distinctive flavors in this memorable dish.

2 beefsteak tomatoes, thinly sliced	
4 leaves fresh basil, finely chopped	
8 pitted black olives, halved	
1 (6 ounce can) tuna, drained	**168 g**
8 slices Swiss cheese	
1 clove garlic, peeled, minced	
2 fillets anchovies, chopped	
5 tablespoons olive oil	**75 ml**
1 tablespoon white vinegar	**15 ml**
16 crackers	
1 teaspoon dried, minced oregano	**5 ml**

- Wash and prepare tomatoes, basil and olives. Set aside. Drain tuna and fluff with fork. Set aside. Slice cheese in shape of crackers.
- In mixing bowl, combine garlic, anchovies, oil and vinegar. Drizzle olive oil mixture onto each cracker.
- Place 1 slice cheese, some tuna, 1 slice tomato and one-half olive on each cracker. Sprinkle with basil and oregano. Drizzle with small amount of olive oil mixture on top.
- Arrange crackers on serving platter to serve.

Serves 4 to 6.

Pomodori Ripieni con Uova e Erbe
(Stuffed Tomatoes with Eggs and Herbs)

This is a truly wonderful starter and is always a hit. It is especially nice and refreshing during the summer months.

4 large beefsteak tomatoes	
1 egg	
2 slices white bread	
1 tablespoon white vinegar	**15 ml**
2 tablespoons chopped parsley	**30 ml**
6 green onions with tops, chopped	
3 tablespoons olive oil	**45 ml**

- Wash tomatoes, cut in half and remove seeds. Set aside.
- Boil egg for about 18 minutes. Peel, chop and set aside.
- Remove crust from bread and soak in vinegar. Mix egg, bread, oil, parsley, onions, salt and pepper to taste.
- Stir to mix well.
- Fill tomatoes with mixture. Chill in refrigerator for about 30 minutes before serving.

Serves 4.

Cipolle Ripiene con Ricotta e Prosciutto

(Stuffed Onions with Ricotta and Prosciutto)

This is an unusual way to prepare onions, but it is oh so good! Cooking the onion brings out the natural sweetness and the prosciutto and ricotta make each bite wonderful.

2 yellow onions, peeled	
½ cup ricotta cheese	**120 ml**
1 tablespoon parmigiano cheese, grated	**15 ml**
2 leaves fresh sage	
1 tablespoon olive oil	**15 ml**
Dash of nutmeg	
2 slices prosciutto	

- Boil onions in salted water for 20 minutes. Remove, rinse under cold water and cut in half horizontally. Remove 1 section inside to allow space for filling. Chop removed section of onion.
- In bowl, mix chopped onion, ricotta, parmigiano, nutmeg, sage, oil, salt and pepper to taste.
- Preheat oven to 350° (176°). Fill onions with mixture. Take 2 slices prosciutto and cut in half. Take 1 slice prosciutto and wrap around each filled onion.
- Place wrapped onions in oven-safe dish coated with olive oil and bake for 20 minutes. Serve warm or cold.

Serves 4.

Insalata di Gorgonzola
(Gorgonzola Salad)

When this sharp Italian cheese combines with crisp, cool pears and sweet red onions, your taste buds will love you.

1 (10 ounce) bag field greens salad mix	**280 g**
½ cup crumbled gorgonzola cheese	**120 ml**
¼ red onion, cut in thin strips	
1 Barlett pear, sliced very thin	
¼ cup shelled walnuts	**60 ml**
3 tablespoons extra-virgin olive oil	**45 ml**
½ tablespoon red wine vinegar	**7 ml**

• In large bowl, combine all ingredients. Toss to mix well. Serve chilled.

Serves 4.

Gorgonzola cheese is a popular sharp Italian cheese that originated in the Middle Ages. It is now produced in the regions of Piedmont and Lombardy in Italy.

Primi Piatti
First Course

Pasta, Minestre, Polenta, Risotto

Pastas, Soups,
Polenta and Risottos

— *per poi passare alla cucina* —

— *Let's move on to the kitchen.* —

Pasta al Pomodoro
(Pasta with Red Tomato Sauce)

This is a classic first course common throughout all regions of Italy and lots of homes in North America.

Sugo di Pomodoro Semplice: (Basic Red Sauce)

2 (28 ounce) cans whole, peeled or crushed tomatoes	**2 (794 g)**
3 tablespoons olive oil	**45 ml**
2 garlic cloves, peeled, minced	
1 teaspoon crushed red pepper	**5 ml**
4 leaves fresh basil	

- Blend tomatoes until smooth. In one large pot, add olive oil and garlic. Sauté garlic until just about golden. Add tomatoes, 2 teaspoons (10 ml) salt, crushed red pepper and basil leaves. Reduce heat to low and simmer for about 1½ hours.

Pasta al Pomodoro:

(Basic Red Sauce - Recipe above)	
1 tablespoon rock salt	**15 ml**
1 (16 ounce) package penne, rigatoni or spaghetti	**.5 kg**
Fresh basil leaves	
Grated parmigiano cheese	

- When the Basic Red Sauce is ready, fill large pot with water and a little rock salt. Bring water to a boil and cook pasta according to package directions.
- Drain pasta and return to pot. Add desired amount of sauce, basil leaves and parmigiano cheese. Serve hot.

Serves 4 to 6.

Tip: Any remaining sauce can be stored in freezer for up to 1 month.

Spaghetti in Salsa Piccante
(Spaghetti with Spicy Sauce)

This spicy, red hot pepper sauce will wake up anyone's senses. It's great for cold, winter nights and warms you up through and through.

3 whole dried red peppers	
2 cloves garlic, peeled, minced	
5 tablespoons olive oil	**75 ml**
2 tablespoons parsley	**30 ml**
1 tablespoon rock salt	**15 ml**
1 (16 ounce) box spaghetti	**.5 kg**
4 tablespoons parmigiano cheese	**60 ml**

- Wash and dry peppers, remove seeds and slice. In blender, add pepper, garlic and 1⅓ cups (320 ml) water. Blend until mixture is smooth.
- In medium skillet, heat half of pepper mixture. Add olive oil, parsley and salt. Cook about 5 minutes.
- Fill large pan with water and rock salt. Bring to boil, add other half of pepper mixture and cook spaghetti according to package directions. Drain pasta, return to pan, add pepper mixture from blender and parmigiano cheese. Serve immediately.

Serves 4 to 6.

There are two varieties of **prezzemolo (parsley)** commonly found at grocery stores and health food markets: curly and flat leaf. The flat leaf variety is known as Italian parsley. It adds a subtle flavor to soups, vegetables, meats and seafood. Since it is a tender herb, it is usually added toward the end of cooking.

Pasta con Melanzane
(Pasta with Eggplant and Red Sauce)

The eggplant is a pleasant addition to classic red sauce.

2 (28 ounce) cans whole peeled or crushed tomatoes	2 (794 g)
3 tablespoons olive oil	45 ml
2 garlic cloves, peeled, minced	
1 large eggplant, cubed	
1 teaspoon crushed red pepper	5 ml
5 fresh basil leaves	
1 tablespoon rock salt	15 ml
1 (16 ounce) box spaghetti pasta	.5 kg
2 cups shredded mozzarella cheese	480 ml
2 tablespoons grated parmigiano cheese, optional	30 ml

- Blend tomatoes until smooth. In large pot, add olive oil, garlic and cubed eggplant and cook until eggplant is tender but firm.
- Add tomatoes, 2 teaspoons (10 ml) salt, crushed red pepper and basil leaves. Reduce heat to low and simmer for about 1½ hours.
- When sauce is ready, fill large pan with water and rock salt. Bring water to boil and cook pasta according to package directions.
- Drain pasta, return to pan and add desired amount of sauce mixture. Add shredded mozzarella cheese and parmigiano cheese (optional) and stir well until cheese melts. Serve hot.

Serves 4 to 6.

Melanzana is the Italian word for eggplant. It continues to be popular in Italian dishes since its introduction by Spaniards in the 1500's.

Pasta con Tonno
(Pasta with Tuna)

Although this recipe may seem like an odd combination of ingredients, it's delicious and is a very popular dish. It's a light, flavorful meal that's even more appealing to the cook because it's so easy to prepare.

1 (28 ounce) can whole peeled or crushed tomatoes	**794 ml**
2 tablespoons olive oil	**30 ml**
¼ cup chopped onion	**60 ml**
1 (6 ounce) can tuna fish, drained	**168 g**
4 fresh basil leaves	
1 tablespoon rock salt	**15 ml**
1 (16 ounce) box spaghetti pasta	**.5 kg**

- Blend tomatoes until smooth. In large pot, add olive oil and chopped onion. Sauté onion until translucent. Add tuna and 1 teaspoon (5 ml) each of salt and pepper.

- Add tomatoes and basil leaves. Reduce heat to low and simmer for about 1½ hours.

- When sauce is ready, fill large pan with water and rock salt. Bring water to boil and cook pasta according to package directions.

- Drain pasta and add desired amount of sauce. Mix well and serve hot.

Serves 4 to 6.

Pasta al Forno
(Oven-Baked Pasta or Mamma's Easy Lasagna)

Mamma makes this recipe quite often because it feeds a large group very easily. She starts simmering the sauce first thing in the morning, then throws the rest together closer to dinnertime. When you're pressed for time, this is an easy version of the Italian classic, lasagna.

Ragú: (Basic Meat Sauce)

2 (28 ounce) cans whole peeled or crushed tomatoes	2 (794 g)
¼ cup chopped onion	60 ml
3 baby carrots, chopped	
½ rib celery, chopped	
3 tablespoons olive oil	45 ml
1 pound lean ground beef or ground turkey	.5 kg
⅓ cup white wine	80 ml
1 teaspoon dried oregano	5 ml
1 cube beef or vegetable bouillon, optional	

- Blend tomatoes until smooth. Chop onion, carrots and celery as small as possible. (In Italy this process is called "battuto".)
- In large pot, add olive oil and "battuto". Sauté until onions are translucent.
- Add ground beef and cook until brown. Add white wine, oregano, 2 teaspoons (10 ml) salt and 1 teaspoon (5 ml) pepper. Add beef or vegetable bouillon cube if desired. Allow wine to cook out.
- Add blended tomatoes. Reduce heat to low and simmer about 2 hours.

(Continued on next page.)

(*Continued*)

Pasta al Forno:

Ragú (Basic Meat Sauce page 32**)**	
1 tablespoon rock salt	**15 ml**
1 (16 ounce) box penne or rigatoni pasta	**.5 kg**
4 cups shredded mozzarella cheese	**.9 ml**
1 cup grated parmigiano cheese	**240 ml**
Besciamella (Basic Bechamel Sauce below)	

- Prepare Ragú (Basic Meat Sauce page 32).
- When Ragú sauce is ready, fill large pan with water and rock salt. Bring water to boil and cook pasta according to package directions.
- Preheat oven to 350° (176°).
- Prepare Besciamella (Basic Bechamel Sauce below).
- Drain pasta, return to pan and add Ragú sauce and parmigiano cheese. Pour into 9 x 13-inch (23 x 33 cm) glass dish. Mix in mozzarella cheese and Besciamella sauce.
- Bake in oven until mozzarella cheese melts, about 15 to 20 minutes. Serve hot.

Serves 4 to 6

Besciamella Sauce: (Basic Bechamel Sauce)

½ cup (1 stick) butter	**120 ml**
4 tablespoons flour	**60 ml**
½ cup milk	**120 ml**
Dash nutmeg	

- Start Besciamella Sauce by melting butter in saucepan and gradually add flour while stirring. Slowly pour milk and continue to stir. (Do not stop stirring or Besciamella will become lumpy.) Add dash of pepper and nutmeg and set aside.

Lasagna

This lasagna is a mouth-watering combination of cheeses, sauces and pasta. The ancient secret to lasagna's success is the creamy, smooth Besciamella Sauce. Just the aroma of lasagna baking in the oven permeates the entire house and brings everyone to the table.

Ragú: (Basic Meat Sauce)

2 (28 ounce) cans whole peeled or crushed tomatoes	2 (794 g)
¼ cup chopped onion	60 ml
3 baby carrots, chopped	
½ rib celery, chopped	
3 tablespoons olive oil	45 ml
1 pound lean ground beef or ground turkey	.5 kg
⅓ cup white wine	80 ml
1 teaspoon dried oregano	5 ml
1 cube beef or vegetable bouillon, optional	

- Blend tomatoes until smooth. Chop onion, carrots and celery as small as possible. (In Italy this process is called "battuto".)
- In large pot, add olive oil and "battuto". Sauté until onions are translucent.
- Add ground beef and cook until brown. Add white wine, oregano, 2 teaspoons (10 ml) salt and 1 teaspoon (5 ml) pepper. Add beef or vegetable bouillon cube if desired. Allow wine to cook out.
- Add blended tomatoes. Reduce heat to low and simmer about 2 hours.

Basic Besciamella Sauce:

½ cup (1 stick) butter	120 ml
4 tablespoons flour	60 ml
½ cup milk	120 ml
Dash nutmeg	

(Continued on next page.)

(*Continued*)

- Start Besciamella Sauce by melting butter in saucepan and gradually add flour while stirring. Slowly pour milk and continue to stir. (Do not stop stirring or besciamella will become lumpy.) Add dash of pepper and nutmeg and set aside.

Lasagna:

Ragú (Basic Meat Sauce page 34**)**	
Besciamella (Basic Bechamel Sauce page 34**)**	
1-2 (9 ounce) boxes lasagna noodles	**1-2 (252 g)**
6 cups shredded mozzarella cheese	**1.5 L**
1 cup grated parmigiano cheese	**240 ml**

- Make Ragú (Basic Meat Sauce page 34).
- Preheat oven to 400° (204°).
- Prepare Besciamella (Basic Bechamel Sauce page 34).
- In 9 x 13-inch (23 x 33 cm) dish, assemble lasagna in alternating layers. Start with layer of ragú sauce, then layer of pasta, followed by more ragu sauce, mozzarella, parmigiano and besciamella.
- Continue layers until dish is full, but not overflowing. Top layer should consist of sauce, mozzarella, parmigiano and Besciamella.
- Place in oven and bake for about 30 to 45 minutes. Remove from oven and set aside for about 5 minutes before cutting and serving.

Serves 4 to 6.

Tip: Sugo di Pomodoro Semplice (Basic Red Sauce) may be used instead of Ragú Sauce. (See page 168.)

> The earliest recorded version of lasagna was in the 13th century and it was described as a layered dish. The earliest versions did not include tomatoes because they had not been discovered by Europeans.

Lasagna di Spinaci
(Spinach Lasagna)

This variation of the classic lasagna uses fresh spinach with lots of mozzarella and parmigiano cheeses. You may also prepare this dish without the spinach.

Sugo di Pomodoro Semplice: (Basic Red Sauce)

2 (28 ounce) cans whole, peeled or crushed tomatoes	**2 (794 g)**
3 tablespoons olive oil	**45 ml**
2 garlic cloves, peeled, minced	
1 teaspoon crushed red pepper	**5 ml**
4 leaves fresh basil	

- Blend tomatoes until smooth. In one large pot, add olive oil and garlic. Sauté garlic until just about golden. Add tomatoes, 2 teaspoons (10 ml) salt, crushed red pepper and basil leaves. Reduce heat to low and simmer for about 1½ hours.

Besciamella Sauce: (Basic Bechamel Sauce)

½ cup (1 stick) butter	**120 ml**
4 tablespoons flour	**60 ml**
½ cup milk	**120 ml**
Dash nutmeg	

- Start Besciamella Sauce by melting butter in saucepan and gradually add flour while stirring. Slowly pour milk and continue to stir. (Do not stop stirring or Besciamella will become lumpy.) Add dash of pepper and nutmeg and set aside.

(Continued on next page.)

(Continued)

Lasagna di Spinaci:

Sugo di Pomodoro Semplice (Basic Red Sauce
  page 36)
Besciamella (Basic Bechamel Sauce page 36)

1-2 (9 ounce) boxes lasagna noodles	**1-2 (252 g)**
2 (5 ounce) packages fresh spinach	**2 (143 g)**
6 cups shredded mozzarella cheese	**1.5 L**
1 cup grated parmigiano cheese	**240 ml**

- Prepare Basic Red Sauce page 36.
- Preheat oven 400° (204°).
- Start Besciamella Sauce page 36.
- Assemble lasagna in 9 x 13-inch (23 x 33 cm) dish. Start with layer of sauce, then layer of pasta (no boiling required), layer of spinach and sprinkle mozzarella, parmigiano and besciamella. Repeat layers until dish is full, but not overflowing. Top layer should consist of sauce, mozzarella, parmigiano and besciamella.
- Place in oven and bake for about 30 to 45 minutes. Remove from oven and set aside for about 5 minutes before cutting and serving.
- Serves 4-6.

Ravioli con Salsicce e Salvia
(Cheese Ravioli with Sausage and Sage)

This is a hearty, robust dish for a complete meal or side dishes. Try pairing this dish with Affetatto Misto (page 10) and Pizza Bianca (page 137). It's a match made in heaven.

4 Italian sausage links	
4 tablespoons (½ stick) butter	**60 ml**
4 leaves fresh sage	
1 tablespoon rock salt	**15 ml**
1 pound pre-packaged cheese ravioli	**.5 kg**
3 tablespoons grated parmigiano cheese	**45 ml**

- Remove casings and crumble sausage. In skillet, melt butter. Add sausage and sauté until sausage cooks thoroughly. Add sage, salt and pepper to taste. Stir to mix well.
- Fill large pot with water and rock salt. Cook ravioli according to package directions.
- Drain and pour ravioli into sausage mixture. Add parmigiano cheese and stir gently. Serve hot.

Serves 4.

Pasta al Ragu: (Pasta with Meat Sauce)

Ragú: (Basic Meat Sauce)

2 (28 ounce) cans whole peeled or crushed tomatoes	**2 (794 g)**
¼ cup chopped onion	**60 ml**
3 baby carrots, chopped	
½ rib celery, chopped	
3 tablespoons olive oil	**45 ml**
1 pound lean ground beef or ground turkey	**.5 kg**
⅓ cup white wine	**80 ml**
1 teaspoon dried oregano	**5 ml**
1 cube beef or vegetable bouillon, optional	

- Blend tomatoes until smooth. Chop onion, carrots and celery as small as possible. (In Italy this process is called "battuto".)
- In large pot, add olive oil and "battuto". Sauté until onions are translucent.
- Add ground beef and cook until brown. Add white wine, oregano, 2 teaspoons (10 ml) salt and 1 teaspoon (5 ml) pepper. Add beef or vegetable bouillon cube if desired. Allow wine to cook out.
- Add blended tomatoes. Reduce heat to low and simmer about 2 hours.

Pasta al Ragu:

Ragú sauce (recipe above)	
1 tablespoon rock salt	**15 ml**
1 (16 ounce) box favorite pasta	**.5 kg**
Grated parmigiano cheese	

- Prepare Basic Meat Sauce (recipe above).
- When sauce is ready, fill large pot with water and rock salt. Bring water to boil and cook pasta according to package directions.
- Drain pasta and add desired amount of Ragú and parmigiano cheese. Serve hot.

Serves 4 to 6.

Tip: Any remaining sauce may be frozen for up to 1 month.

Pennette al Pomodoro e Vodka
(Mini-Penne Pasta with Tomato and Vodka)

Don't worry about the alcohol in this recipe. It cooks down, cannot be tasted, but it brings out the flavors of the sauce.

2 beefsteak tomatoes	
2 tablespoons olive oil	**30 ml**
1 clove garlic, peeled, crushed	
⅓ cup sliced bacon	**80 ml**
2 tablespoons vodka	**30 ml**
1 tablespoon rock salt	**15 ml**
1 (16 ounce) box mini-penne pasta	**.5 kg**
1 tablespoon chopped fresh parsley	**15 ml**

- Wash, peel and slice tomatoes into small cubes. Combine olive oil and garlic in skillet. Cook on high heat for about 1 minute.

- Add bacon, reduce heat and cook for about 1 minute. Remove garlic and discard. Add vodka and allow it to cook for 1 minute. Add tomatoes and cook for 1 additional minute. Add salt and pepper to taste.

- Fill large pot with water and rock salt. Bring to boil and cook pasta according to package directions. Drain pasta and add to skillet with sauce. Stir to mix well. Garnish with parsley and serve.

Serves 4 to 6.

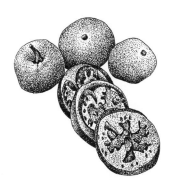

Pasta Carbonara
(Pasta with Egg and Bacon)

1 tablespoon rock salt	15 ml
1 (16 ounce) box penne or rigatoni pasta	.5 kg
8-10 slices bacon, cut into small pieces	
3 eggs	
1/3 cup heavy whipping cream	80 ml
1/4 cup grated parmigiano cheese	60 ml

- Fill large pot with water and rock salt. Bring water to boil and cook pasta according to package directions.
- Brown bacon pieces over medium heat in skillet until thoroughly cooked. Drain excess fat and set aside.
- In medium bowl, whisk eggs, salt and pepper to taste.
- Drain pasta and return to pot. Place pot over low heat. Add egg mixture and mix well with large wooden spoon until eggs appear cooked. Add bacon, whipping cream and parmigiano cheese and continue to stir until they mix. Serve hot.

Serves 4 to 6.

Tip: It's very important to cook pasta al dente because it continues to cook a bit longer with the carbonara sauce.

Carbonara is a very popular, tasty and easy-to-prepare Roman dish. The origin of this traditional recipe is uncertain, but there are plenty of stories that attempt to explain its history. Alla carbonara means "in the manner of the charcoal men". It is believed that either this dish was originally made for charcoal makers or made over a charcoal grill. Some other stories suggest that this dish was made for the carbonari who were members of a secret Italian society. No matter what the true story is, the union of eggs, bacon and pasta is pure genius.

Fettucine con Spinaci
(Fettucine with Spinach)

This is a delicious, vegetarian-friendly dish. We love to combine vegetables and pasta into one dish.

1 cup fresh spinach	**240 ml**
2 eggs	
3 tablespoons grated parmigiano cheese	**45 ml**
4 slices prosciutto	
2 tablespoons olive oil	**30 ml**
1 tablespoon rock salt	**15 ml**
1(16 ounce) box fettucine	**.5 kg**

- Wash and dry spinach and set aside. In separate bowl, whisk eggs with salt and pepper to taste. Add parmigiano and spinach into egg mixture and set aside.

- Slice proscuitto into thick strips. In large, non-stick skillet, combine olive oil and prosciutto and cook over medium heat for about 2 to 3 minutes or until crunchy.

- Fill large pot with water and add rock salt. Bring water to boil, add pasta and cook according to package directions.

- Remove 2 tablespoons (30 ml) boiling water and add to egg mixture. Drain pasta and place in skillet with proscuitto. Pour egg mixture over it and mix well. Serve immediately.

Serves 4 to 6.

Pasta con Melanzane e Ricotta
(Pasta with Eggplant and Ricotta)

This particular dish is a perfect example of the versatility of pasta. The fresh flavors of the eggplant and the smoothness of the ricotta make this a truly remarkable experience!

3 ripe tomatoes	
1 medium eggplant	
1 tablespoon rock salt	**15 ml**
1 (16 ounce) box farfalle pasta	**.5 kg**
½ cup olive oil	**120 ml**
1 clove garlic, peeled, minced	
1 teaspoon crushed red pepper	**5 ml**
1 cup ricotta cheese, drained	**240 ml**
3 leaves fresh basil	

- Clean, peel and cut tomatoes into cubes. Cut eggplant into cubes. Set aside.
- Fill large pot with water and add rock salt. Bring water to boil and cook pasta according to package directions.
- While water boils, prepare skillet with olive oil, garlic and crushed red pepper. Add vegetables and sauté for about 10 minutes.
- Remove from heat. Allow mixture to cool for 10 minutes. Add ricotta and basil leaves and stir to mix well.
- Drain pasta, return to pot and add ricotta mixture. Stir to mix well and serve hot.

Serves 4 to 6.

Pasta Contadína
(Peasant Pasta)

What a traditional recipe from Tuscany! This dish gets its name from the old concept of using whatever ingredients are in the pantry. Leave it to Italian grandmothers to create a fabulous dish with whatever they have on hand.

1 (16 ounce) box penne pasta	.5 kg
1 tablespoon rock salt	15 ml
¼ cup (½ stick) butter	60 ml
¼ cup finely chopped onion	60 ml
4 slices ham, diced	
6 ounces fresh mushrooms, sliced	168 g
1 cup frozen peas	240 ml
Heavy whipping cream, optional	
Grated parmigiano cheese	

- Fill large pot with water and add rock salt. Bring water to boil and cook pasta according to package directions.
- In medium skillet, melt butter, add finely chopped onions and cook until translucent.
- Add ham, mushrooms and peas. Mix well and add salt and pepper to taste.
- Continue to cook on low heat for about 15 minutes. (If you use cream, add at this point and continue cooking for 2 minutes.)
- Drain pasta and return to pot. Add sauce and stir thoroughly. Garnish with parmigiano cheese and serve hot.

Serves 4 to 6.

Fettucine Paglia e Fieno
(Rustic Fettucine)

This colorful and unique dish combines spinach fettuccine and traditional fettuccine. The literal translation for this recipe is "straw and hay".

3 tablespoons olive oil	45 ml
2 cloves fresh garlic, peeled, crushed	
1 teaspoon crushed red pepper	5 ml
2 portabella mushrooms, sliced	
½ cup sliced fresh mushrooms	120 ml
2 tablespoons chopped fresh parsley	30 ml
½ (16 ounce) box spinach fettucine	.5 kg
½ (16 ounce) box fettucine	.5 kg
1 tablespoon rock salt	15 ml

- In large skillet over medium heat, combine olive oil, garlic and crushed red pepper. Add mushrooms and parsley.
- Cook for about 10 minutes or until mushrooms are tender. Cover and reduce heat to low.
- Fill large pot with water and add rock salt. Bring water to boil and cook pasta according to package directions. Drain pasta and add mushroom mixture. Stir to mix well. Serve hot.

Serves 4.

Farfalle con Funghi e Ricotta
(Farfalle with Mushroom and Ricotta)

Ricotta is a fine, delicate cheese and its subtle taste blends well with the earthy flavor of mushrooms. This a superb dish for your family and friends.

3 tablespoons butter	**45 ml**
3 cloves fresh garlic, peeled, crushed	
2 cups sliced fresh mushrooms	**480 ml**
2 cups fresh ricotta, drained	**480 ml**
½ cup half-and-half cream	**120 ml**
2 tablespoons parmigiano cheese	**30 ml**
1 (16 ounce) box farfalle pasta	**.5 kg**
1 tablespoon rock salt	**15 ml**
1 tablespoon fresh parsley	**15 ml**

- In skillet over medium heat, combine butter, garlic, mushrooms, salt and pepper to taste.
- In separate mixing bowl, combine ricotta cheese and half-and-half and stir until smooth and creamy. Add parmigiano cheese.
- Fill large pot with water and add rock salt. Bring water to boil and cook pasta according to package directions.
- Drain pasta and place in individual serving bowls. Pour desired amount of ricotta mixture on each serving of pasta, then pour desired amount of mushroom mixture. Garnish with parsley and serve immediately.

Serves 4 to 6.

Pasta Aglio e Olio
(Pasta with Garlic and Olive Oil)

This is as simple as it gets. It is the true taste of home and is best known for being one of Italy's leading "comfort foods"! In all Italian homes, Neopolitan in particular, this dish is considered a quick dinner, late night snack or even a digestive. No matter the occasion, this dish is a must to sample.

1 (16 ounce) box spaghetti pasta	**.5 kg**
1 tablespoon rock salt	**15 ml**
5 tablespoons olive oil	**75 ml**
2 garlic cloves, peeled, minced	
2-3 teaspoons crushed red pepper	**10-15 ml**
2 tablespoons fresh parsley, finely chopped	**30 ml**

- Fill large pot with water and rock salt. Bring water to boil and cook pasta according to package directions.
- In medium saucepan, combine olive oil, garlic, crushed red pepper and salt. Cook on medium heat until garlic is just about golden. (DO NOT cook on high heat or garlic will burn.)
- Drain pasta and return to pot. Stir in sauce and parsley. Mix well and serve immediately.

Serves 4 to 6.

Bucatini alla Matriciana
(Bucatini Pasta with Red Sauce and Bacon)

This is a very popular pasta. It is an authentic recipe originating from Amatrice, a small village in the province of Rieti. The red sauce may be omitted to create a variation called pasta alla grecia, a typical dish of the Abruzzi region when Amatrice was part of the province L'Aquila.

1 (28 ounce) can whole, peeled or crushed tomatoes	794 g
2 tablespoons olive oil	30 ml
¼ cup finely chopped onion	60 ml
4-6 slices pancetta	
1 teaspoon crushed red pepper	5 ml
3 fresh basil leaves	
1 (16 ounce) box bucatini pasta	.5 kg
1 tablespoon rock salt	15 ml

- Blend tomatoes until smooth. In large pot, add olive oil and onion. Sauté until onions are translucent.
- Add pancetta or bacon and cook thoroughly. (If cooking bacon or pancetta directly in olive oil, amount of olive oil should be reduced due to some fat from pancetta or bacon.)
- Add tomatoes, 1 teaspoon (5 ml) salt, crushed red pepper and basil leaves. Reduce heat to low and simmer for about 1½ hours.
- Fill large pot with water and add rock salt. Bring water to boil and cook pasta according to package directions.
- Drain pasta and return to pot. Add pasta and desired amount of sauce. Mix thoroughly and serve immediately.

Serves 4 to 6.

Tip: For a healthier way of eating, cook pancetta or bacon in a separate skillet. Drain all fat and add to the sauce. You may substitute bacon for pancetta.

Orecchiette con Broccoli
(Orecchiette with Broccoli)

Orecchiette is an unusually shaped pasta resembling tiny ears. This vegetarian dish can easily be paired with a fresh salad and Pizza Bianca for a wonderful meal.

1 (16 ounce) box orecchiette pasta	**.5 kg**
1 tablespoon rock salt	**15 ml**
3 cups broccoli florets, fresh or frozen	**710 ml**
2 tablespoons olive oil	**30 ml**
2 garlic cloves, peeled, minced	
1 teaspoon crushed red pepper	**5 ml**

- Fill large pot with water and add rock salt. Bring water to boil and cook pasta according to package directions.
- While pasta boils, steam broccoli about 5 to 7 minutes. Drain and set aside.
- In medium skillet, combine olive oil, garlic and crushed red pepper. Cook over medium to low heat until garlic is just about golden.
- Add broccoli and 1 teaspoon (5 ml) salt and sauté over medium heat for about 10 minutes. Broccoli should be tender.
- Drain pasta and add broccoli mixture. Serve hot.

Serves 4 to 6.

Pasta con Carciofi
(Pasta with Artichokes)

Vegetables are a very important part of the Mediterranean diet. This recipe uses artichokes combined with two delicious Italian cheeses.

1 (16 ounce) box rigatoni pasta	.5 kg
1 tablespoon rock salt	15 ml
3 tablespoons olive oil	45 ml
¼ cup finely chopped onion	60 ml
2 tablespoons pecorino cheese	30 ml
2 tablespoons parmigiano cheese	30 ml
1 (14 ounce) can artichoke hearts, drained	396 g

- Fill large pot with water and add rock salt. Bring water to boil and cook pasta according to package directions.
- In medium skillet, combine olive oil, onions and artichokes. Sauté over medium heat for about 5 to 8 minutes. Add pecorino and parmigiano cheese.
- Drain pasta and return to pot. Add artichoke mixture, salt and pepper to taste and stir to mix well.

Serves 4 to 6.

Pennette al Salmone
(Mini-Penne Pasta with Salmon Sauce)

Salmon is a very popular ingredient in pasta sauces. It gives this recipe a subtle, yet forceful flavor. Add pasta immediately after sauce cooks.

1 (16 ounce) box pennette or mini-penne pasta	.5 kg
1 tablespoon rock salt	15 ml
2 tablespoons butter	30 ml
1 (4 ounce) package smoked salmon	114 g
1 (28 ounce) can whole peeled or crushed tomatoes	794 g
⅓ cup heavy whipping cream	80 ml
1 tablespoon finely chopped parsley	15 ml

- Fill large pot with water and add rock salt. Bring water to boil and cook pasta according to package directions.
- In medium saucepan, melt butter, add thinly sliced salmon and sauté over medium heat for about 7 minutes. Add tomatoes, reduce heat, cover and simmer for about 1 hour.
- Add whipping cream, salt and pepper to taste and mix well.
- Drain pasta, return to pot and add salmon mixture and parsley. Stir to mix well and serve hot.

Serves 4.

Around the 16th century, Europeans were introduced to the **tomato** after explorers returned from China with the fruit. From this time to today, Italians continue to use tomatoes in extraordinary ways.

Pennette con Gamberi e Verdure
(Mini-Penne Pasta with Shrimp and Vegetables)

This is a simple, refreshing, heart-healthy dish from the pages of an old Italian food magazine. The delicious combination of pasta with fresh vegetables and shrimp is difficult to top.

1 (16 ounce) box pennette or mini-penne pasta	**.5 kg**
1 tablespoon rock salt	**15 ml**
2 tablespoons olive oil	**30 ml**
1 teaspoon crushed red pepper	**5 ml**
½ cup sliced baby carrots	**120 ml**
¼ cup finely chopped onion	**60 ml**
4 small zucchini, sliced	
1 pound fresh or frozen shrimp, peeled, veined	**.5 kg**

- Fill large pot with water and add rock salt. Bring water to boil and cook pasta according to package directions.
- Combine olive oil, 1 teaspoon (5 ml) salt, crushed red pepper, carrots, onion and zucchini in skillet. Sauté vegetables for 15 to 20 minutes over medium heat until vegetables firm, but cooked. Add shrimp and cook until shrimp turns pink.
- Drain pasta, return to pot and add shrimp mixture. Stir to mix well and serve hot.

Serves 4 to 6.

Pasta alla Sorrentina
(Sorrento Pasta)

This colorful pasta dish reflects the beauty of Sorrento, the town for which it is named.

1 (16 ounce) box pasta	.5 kg
1 tablespoon rock salt	15 ml
3 tablespoons olive oil	45 ml
2 cloves garlic, peeled, crushed	
1 pound fresh or frozen shrimp, peeled, veined	.5 kg
6-8 cherry tomatoes, halved	
1 tablespoon chopped fresh parsley	15 ml

- Fill large pot with water and add rock salt. Bring water to boil and cook pasta according to package directions.
- Heat olive oil and garlic over medium heat in skillet. Add shrimp and cook for about 5 minutes or until shrimp turn pink.
- Add tomatoes, parsley, salt and pepper to taste. Stir to mix well.
- Drain pasta, return to pot and add shrimp mixture. Stir to mix well and serve hot.

Serves 4 to 6.

Sorrento is a well-known resort in southern Italy perched on top steeply rising cliffs and overlooking the bay of Naples. Sorrento has been a popular vacation retreat since at least 600 AD. According to early Greek legend, it was at Sorrento that Ulysses heard the tempting song of the sirens, the nymphs who labored long hours to seduce and shipwreck passing sailors.

Polenta
(Cornmeal Dish)

Polenta is a tradition of the regions of Friuli and Veneto. This versatile grain can be prepared and served soft, hard, grilled or fried. It can also be topped with virtually anything. The polenta in this recipe is dressed with our classic Ragú Sauce.

Ragú: (Basic Meat Sauce)

2 (28 ounce) cans whole peeled or crushed tomatoes	2 (794 g)
¼ cup chopped onion	60 ml
3 baby carrots, chopped	
½ rib celery, chopped	
3 tablespoons olive oil	45 ml
1 pound lean ground beef or ground turkey	.5 kg
⅓ cup white wine	80 ml
1 teaspoon dried oregano	5 ml
1 cube beef or vegetable bouillon, optional	

- Blend tomatoes until smooth. Chop onion, carrots and celery as small as possible. (In Italy this process is called "battuto".)
- In large pot, add olive oil and "battuto". Sauté until onions are translucent.
- Add ground beef and cook until brown. Add white wine, oregano, 2 teaspoons (10 ml) salt and 1 teaspoon (5 ml) pepper. Add beef or vegetable bouillon cube if desired. Allow wine to cook out.
- Add blended tomatoes. Reduce heat to low and simmer about 2 hours.

(Continued on next page.)

(*Continued*)

Polenta:

Basic Meat Sauce (page 54)
8 cups water   1.9 L
2 tablespoons olive oil   30 ml
2½ cups polenta   600 ml
Grated parmigiano cheese

- Prepare Basic Meat Sauce (page 54).
- When Basic Meat Sauce is ready, combine water and a little salt in a large pot. When water boils, add olive oil and polenta. Stir slowly with wooden spoon. Cook for about 20 minutes and stir occasionally.
- Remove from heat and pour polenta on serving platter or serving bowls. Pour sauce over polenta and sprinkle with parmigiano cheese. Serve hot.

Serves 6.

Polenta al Forno
(Baked Polenta with Italian Cheeses)

This is truly the staple food of northern Italy where it still outshines pasta. This baked cheesy alternative will absolutely delight any palate.

8 cups water	**1.9 L**
2 tablespoons olive oil	**30 ml**
2½ cups polenta	**600 ml**
¼ cup grated fontina cheese	**60 ml**
¼ cup grated mozzarella cheese	**60 ml**
¼ cup provolone cheese	**60 ml**
Parmigiano cheese	

- Preheat oven to 350° (176°). In large pot, combine water and 1 tablespoon (15 ml) salt. When water boils, add olive oil and polenta package contents. Stir slowly with wooden spoon. Cook about 20 minutes and stir occasionally. Remove from heat and set aside.

- Prepare 9 x 13-inch (23 x 33 cm) dish with non-stick spray. Pour polenta into dish and add cheeses. Bake about 20 minutes or until cheese is bubbly and polenta edges are golden brown.

- Remove from oven and allow it to sit for a few minutes before cutting and serving.

- Serve hot and enjoy!

Serves 6.

Polenta Fritta
(Fried Polenta)

It is a universal law that anything fried has to be good. Well, polenta is no exception! This version is great served as a side dish or enjoyed as a main course.

8 cups water	**1.9 L**
2 tablespoons olive oil	**30 ml**
2½ cups polenta	**600 ml**
Cooking oil for frying	
Parmigiano cheese	

- Combine water and a little salt in large pot. When water boils, add olive oil and polenta. Stir slowly with wooden spoon. Cook about 20 minutes and stir occasionally
- Remove from heat and set aside to cool. Polenta should be completely cool before cutting.
- In large non-stick skillet, heat cooking oil. Cut polenta into 3 x 3-inch (8 x 8 cm) squares.
- When oil is hot, add polenta and reduce heat. Fry well on both sides and turn occasionally.
- Remove when polenta is golden brown and set on paper towels to drain before serving. Garnish with parmigiano cheese and serve hot.

Serves 6.

Risotto al Sugo di Carne
Ragú Risotto

This recipe is a little more involved, but well worth the effort. Once you try this recipe, you see that the risotto served in a restaurant will rarely compare to a good homemade risotto.

Ragú: (Basic Meat Sauce, page 59)

2 (28 ounce) cans whole peeled or crushed tomatoes	**2 (794 g)**
¼ cup chopped onion	**60 ml**
3 baby carrots, chopped	
½ rib celery, chopped	
3 tablespoons olive oil	**45 ml**
1 pound lean ground beef or ground turkey	**.5 kg**
⅓ cup white wine	**80 ml**
1 teaspoon dried oregano	**5 ml**
1 cube beef or vegetable bouillon, optional	

- Blend tomatoes until smooth. Chop onion, carrots and celery as small as possible. (In Italy this process is called "battuto".)
- In large pot, add olive oil and "battuto". Sauté until onions are translucent.
- Add ground beef and cook until brown. Add white wine, oregano, 2 teaspoons (10 ml) salt and 1 teaspoon (5 ml) pepper. Add beef or vegetable bouillon cube if desired. Allow wine to cook out.
- Add blended tomatoes. Reduce heat to low and simmer about 2 hours.

(Continued on next page.)

(Continued)

Risotto al Sugo di Carne:

Basic Meat Sauce (page 58)	
8 cups water	**1.9 L**
1 tablespoon rock salt	**15 ml**
2 cups Arborio rice or medium-grain rice	**480 ml**
Parmigiano cheese	

- Prepare Basic Meat Sauce (page 58).
- When Basic Meat Sauce is ready, combine water and a little salt in a large pot Bring to boil, add rice and cook according to package directions.
- Drain risotto, return to pot and add sauce. Stir to mix well and garnish with parmigiano cheese.

Serves 4 to 6.

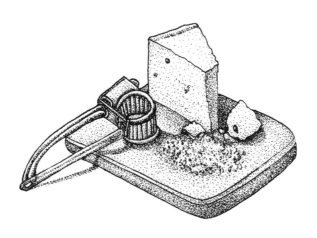

Riso al Burro e Parmigiano
(Parmigiano Risotto)

Making a good risotto takes a little bit of practice and concentration to get the timing right, but this is a good recipe for beginners.

6 cups beef, vegetable or chicken stock	**1.5 L**
6 tablespoons butter	**90 ml**
1 small onion, finely chopped	
2 cups Arborio rice or other medium-grain rice	**480 ml**
¾ cup white wine	**180 ml**
1 cup grated parmigiano cheese	**240 ml**

- In small pan, heat broth over medium heat and keep warm until ready to use.
- In skillet, melt butter over medium heat and add onions. Sauté onions until they are translucent. Add rice and stir to mix well.
- After 2 minutes, add wine. Allow wine to cook out. Begin adding broth slowly and stir frequently. Add salt and pepper to taste. Stir to mix well. Risotto should cook about 20 to 30 minutes or until al dente.
- Remove from heat and add parmigiano. Stir to mix well. Serve hot.

Serves 4 to 6.

Risotto con Verdure
(Vegetable Risotto)

Risotto is very popular in Milan and other Italian regions. There are hundreds of risotto varying with flavoring ingredients used. This vegetable variation is nutritious and fairly simple to prepare.

1 tablespoon rock salt	15 ml
2 cups Arborio rice or medium-grain rice	480 ml
2 ripe tomatoes	
1 yellow pepper	
2 small zucchini	
1 small eggplant	
3 tablespoons olive oil	45 ml
1 clove garlic, peeled	
¼ cup (½ stick) butter	60 ml
1 cube vegetable bouillon	
¼ cup chopped onion	60 ml
¼ cup chopped celery	60 ml
½ cup white wine	120 ml
4 tablespoons grated parmigiano cheese	60 ml

- In large pot combine 6 cups (1.5 L) water and a little salt. Bring to boil, add rice and cook according to package directions. Drain and set aside.
- Wash vegetables and cut into small pieces. Set aside.
- In skillet, heat olive oil and garlic. Remove and discard. Add tomatoes, peppers, eggplant and zucchini.
- Cook over medium heat about 10 minutes. Remove from heat and set aside.
- Melt butter with vegetable bouillon in separate pot. Add chopped onions and celery and cook until onions are translucent. Add wine and continue to cook about 5 minutes.
- Remove from heat. Add rice, salt and pepper to taste and stir to mix well. Place pot back on very low heat and add vegetable mixture. Stir to mix well. Add parmigiano cheese and serve.

Serves 4.

Pomodori Ripieni
(Stuffed Tomatoes)

This is one of many traditional Roman dishes that deserves to be mentioned. The secret of the success of this dish is the type of tomatoes used. The tomatoes cannot be too ripe or too hard or they will not cook well.

Sugo di Pomodoro Semplice: (Basic Red Sauce)

2 (28 ounce) cans whole, peeled or crushed tomatoes	2 (794 g)
3 tablespoons olive oil	45 ml
2 garlic cloves, peeled, minced	
1 teaspoon crushed red pepper	5 ml
4 leaves fresh basil	

- Blend tomatoes until smooth. In one large pot, add olive oil and garlic. Sauté garlic until just about golden. Add tomatoes, 2 teaspoons (10 ml) salt, crushed red pepper and basil leaves. Reduce heat to low and simmer for about 1½ hours.

Pomodori Ripieni:

Basic Red Sauce (Recipe above)	
6 large beefsteak tomatoes	
3 cups Arborio or basmati rice	710 ml
4 tablespoons olive oil	60 ml
⅓ cup grated parmigiano cheese	80 ml

- Prepare Basic Red Sauce (recipe above).
- When Basic Red Sauce is ready, preheat oven to 375° (190°).
- Wash tomatoes. Cut large hole in top of tomato. Remove pulp and seeds.
- Cook rice according to package directions.
- Drain rice and return to pot. Add sauce, olive oil, parmigiano cheese and mix well.
- Scoop rice mixture into tomatoes and fill to top loosely.
- Prepare oven-safe dish with non-stick spray. Place tomatoes in dish and bake about 20 to 30 minutes. Remove from oven and serve hot.

Serves 4 to 6.

Peperoni Ripieni
(Stuffed Bell Pepper)

The concept of stuffed peppers and its variations is endless. In this recipe, we stuff the peppers with meat and a host of other flavorful ingredients. It makes a unique, hearty dish.

6 large bell peppers	
1 pound lean ground beef	**.5 kg**
1 egg	
4 tablespoons plus 1 tablespoon plain breadcrumbs, divided	**60 ml**
1 tablespoon finely chopped fresh parsley	**15 ml**
2 tablespoons grated parmigiano cheese	**30 ml**
Dash of nutmeg	
3 tablespoons olive oil	**45 ml**
¼ cup finely chopped onion	**60 ml**
4-6 baby carrots, finely chopped	
½ cup white wine	**120 ml**
1 cube vegetable bouillon	

- Wash peppers and cut large hole on top. Remove seeds and set peppers aside.
- In separate dish, combine ground beef, egg, breadcrumbs, parsley, parmigiano cheese, salt and pepper to taste and nutmeg. Mix well.
- Fill peppers with meat mixture and pack loosely. Once filled, sprinkle remaining breadcrumbs on top of meat mixture.
- In large pot, combine olive oil, onions and carrots. Sauté until onions are translucent. Place peppers in pot standing up.
- Cover and simmer about 15 minutes. Add wine, cover and simmer over low heat about 45 minutes or until meat cooks thoroughly.
- If liquid reduces too much, vegetable stock may be added during cooking time. Place 1 cup (240 ml) water with vegetable bouillon in microwave to create a vegetable stock.

Serves 4 to 6.

TIP: If peppers are too large to stand up, place them on their side. Be sure to turn them often to cook on all sides.

Pasta e Fagioli
(Bean Soup)

Pasta fagioli has become a universal "comfort" soup with many different variations according to the regions. This recipe uses red kidney beans just as the Romans do it.

3 tablespoons olive oil	**45 ml**
2 baby carrots, finely chopped	
¼ cup finely chopped onions	**60 ml**
1 slice bacon	
2 (16 ounce) cans red kidney beans, divided	**2 (.5 kg)**
1 sprig fresh rosemary	
1 (16 ounce) package tubini pasta	**.5 kg**
Grated parmigiano cheese	

- In large, deep pot, combine olive oil, carrots and onions. Sauté until onions are translucent. Add slice of bacon.
- Drain 1 can beans and add to pot with rosemary, salt and pepper to taste. Stir to mix well.
- Place other can of beans with its juice in blender and puree. Add to pot.
- Cover and simmer over low heat about 25 minutes. Check periodically and stir.
- Add 4 cups (.9 L) water and bring to boil. Add pasta and cook pasta according to package directions.
- Before serving, remove bacon and garnish with parmigiano cheese. Serve hot.

Serves 4 to 6.

Tip: If you use dried beans, be sure to soak them overnight. Pasta may be omitted from this recipe if desired.

Pasta e Patate
(Broth-Based Potato Soup)

Pasta e patate was known as peasant soup during the world wars because it was so inexpensive to make. To this day, Italians enjoy this delicious dish and you and your family will too.

3 tablespoons olive oil	**45 ml**
2 baby carrots, finely chopped	
¼ cup finely chopped onion	**60 ml**
1 slice bacon	
4 large Yukon potatoes, cubed	
1 sprig fresh rosemary	
1 cube vegetable bouillon	
1 (16 ounce) package tubini pasta	**.5 kg**
Grated parmigiano cheese	

- In large, deep pot, combine olive oil, carrots and onions. Sauté until onions are translucent. Add slice of bacon. NOTE: Once soup is ready to serve, the bacon will be removed.
- Add potatoes, rosemary, salt and pepper to taste and vegetable bouillon. Stir to mix well.
- Cover and simmer on low heat about 30 minutes. Check periodically and stir.
- Add 4 cups (.9 L) water and bring to boil. Add pasta and cook according to directions on box.
- Remove bacon, garnish with parmigiano cheese and serve hot.

Serves 4 to 6.

Tip: Pasta may be omitted from this recipe if desired.

Pasta e Ceci
(Chickpea Soup)

Pasta e Ceci is not as well known as its cousin Pasta e Fagiolini. In the Marche region of Italy, the tradition is to prepare Pasta e Ceci during harvest in hopes the wheat would be the size of chickpeas.

3 tablespoons olive oil	**45 ml**
2 baby carrots, finely chopped	
¼ cup finely chopped onion	**60 ml**
2 (16 ounce) cans chickpeas	**2 (.5 kg)**
1 sprig fresh rosemary	
1 cube vegetable bouillon	
1 (16 ounce) package tubini pasta	**.5 kg**
Grated parmigiano cheese	

- In large, deep pot, combine olive oil, carrots and onions. Sauté until onions are translucent.
- Add chickpeas, rosemary, salt and pepper to taste and vegetable bouillon. Stir to mix well.
- Cover and simmer on low heat about 30 minutes. Check periodically and stir.
- Add 4 cups (.9 L) water and bring to boil. Add pasta and cook according to package directions. Garnish with parmigiano cheese and serve hot.

Serves 4 to 6.

Tip: Pasta may be omitted from this recipe if desired.

Minestra di Lenticchie
(Lentil Soup)

The legend is that if, Minestra di Lenticchie is eaten in large quantities on New Year's Eve, health, happiness and prosperity will be the rewards. Eating this soup is a reward in itself.

½ **pound dried lentils**	**227 g**
3 tablespoons olive oil	**45 ml**
2 baby carrots, whole	
1 slice bacon	
2 garlic cloves, peeled, crushed	
2 teaspoons crushed red pepper	**10 ml**
2 cups crushed tomatoes	**480 ml**
1 cube vegetable bouillon	
1 (16 ounce) package tubini pasta	**.5 kg**
Grated parmigiano cheese	

- Wash, drain lentils and set aside.
- In large, deep pot, combine olive oil, carrots, bacon, garlic, crushed red pepper, salt to taste, tomatoes and vegetable bouillon. Sauté about 10 minutes.
- Add lentils and 1 cup (240 ml) water. Cover and simmer about 30 minutes.
- Add 4 cups (.9 L) water and bring to boil. Add pasta and cook according to package directions. Garnish with parmigiano cheese and serve hot.

Serves 4 to 6.

Tip: Pasta may be omitted from this recipe if desired.

Minestrone
(Vegetable Soup with Pasta)

Minestrone is a rustic country soup that takes a little time to prepare, but the results are worth it. Any combination of fresh vegetables in season may be used to create this nutritious recipe.

2 small potatoes, cubed	
1 cup broccoli florets	**240 ml**
1 cup cauliflower florets	**240 ml**
1 cup sliced carrots	**240 ml**
3 small zucchini, sliced	
1 cup green beans	**240 ml**
3 tablespoons olive oil	**45 ml**
¼ cup chopped onion	**60 ml**
1 cube beef, vegetable or chicken bouillon	
Grated parmigiano cheese	

- Wash vegetables and set aside.
- In large, deep pot, heat olive oil and onions and cook until onions are translucent. Add all vegetables, salt and pepper to taste and stir to mix well.
- Add 10 cups (2.5 L) water and bouillon. Reduce heat to low and cover. Stir periodically.
- Cook about 30 to 40 minutes or until vegetables are tender.
- If mixture is too dense before adding pasta, add water. Bring to boil and cook pasta according to package directions. Garnish with parmigiano cheese and serve hot. Serves 4 to 6.

Tip: A variation of this soup is to blend vegetables before adding. Pasta may be omitted from this recipe if desired.

Tortellini in Brodo
(Tortellini in Broth)

The Bolognesi claim the creation of this ring-shaped, filled pasta. It is said that when the Bolognesi eat Tortellini in Brodo, they never speak a word until the dish is finished and then only to utter a word of appreciation.

3 tablespoons olive oil	**45 ml**
½ whole onion	
1 rib celery, halved	
6 whole baby carrots	
½ whole chicken, boned, cut into pieces	
1 cube vegetable bouillon	
1 (8 ounce) package tortellini	**227 g**
Grated parmigiano cheese	

- Fill large pot with 10 cups (2.5 L) water and all ingredients, except tortellini and parmigiano cheese. Bring to boil, cover, reduce heat and simmer for 45 minutes or until chicken cooks through.
- Remove chicken and vegetables and set aside.
- Bring broth to boil. Add tortellini and cook according to package directions. Serve hot and garnish with parmigiano cheese.

Serves 4.

Tip: Chicken and vegetables may be served on the side garnished with mayonnaise, salt and pepper.

Pasta al Limone
(Lemon Pasta)

This pasta dish is delicious and fast. It's great for a light meal or as a starter for a seafood dinner.

½ **cup olive oil**	**120 ml**
2 cloves garlic, minced	
1 cup fresh parsley, minced	**240 ml**
3 lemons	
¾ **cup pine nuts**	**180 ml**
1 (16 ounce) box spaghetti or fettucine	**.5 kg**
1 tablespoon rock salt	**15 ml**

- Combine olive oil, garlic, parsley and juice of 2 lemons in large bowl. Season with salt and pepper. Add pine nuts and stir to mix well. Set aside for a couple of hours and allow flavors to blend thoroughly.

- Fill large pot with water and rock salt. Bring water to boil and cook pasta according to package directions. Before draining, save 1 small cup (240 ml) pasta water.

- Drain pasta and return it to pot. Pour lemon sauce over pasta and cook over high heat. Add some of reserved pasta water to prevent it from drying out.

- Continue to cook until pasta and sauce are hot. Remove from heat and serve. (Be sure to scrape any remaining pine nuts from bottom of pot to top of pasta.) Serve this dish with lemon wedges.

Serves 4 to 6.

Secondi Piatti
Second Course

— E adesso passiamo alle cose serie…Quindi, preparatevi! —

— And now let's move on to the serious food…So, let's get ready! —

Pollo al Forno con Patate
(Oven-Baked Chicken with Roasted Potatoes)

This is an easy way to put together a complete meal. Oven roasting does wonders for chicken and this recipe is no exception. It has a very mellow flavor and is exceptionally juicy. The golden brown, crispy potatoes make this a must to try.

4 large potatoes, peeled, cubed	
1 whole chicken	
3 tablespoons olive oil, divided	**45 ml**
1 teaspoon minced garlic	**5 ml**
2 sprigs fresh rosemary	

- Preheat oven to 375° (190° C).
- Wash, peel and cube potatoes and set aside. Wash chicken thoroughly.
- In oven-safe dish, combine 1 tablespoon (15 ml) olive oil and garlic. Place potatoes in dish and coat with 2 tablespoons (30 ml) olive oil. Add chicken and sprinkle rosemary, salt and pepper to taste evenly over chicken and potatoes.
- Cook about 1 to 1½ hours or until chicken is well done. Stir potatoes occasionally

Serves 4.

Zucchine Ripiene con Patate
(Stuffed Zucchini with Roasted Potatoes)

Zucchini owes its name to the type developed in Italy "zucca" meaning marrow and "ini" meaning little. All summer squashes are considered marrow squashes because the insides are edible.

6 large zucchini	
4 large potatoes	
1 pound lean ground beef or turkey	**.5 kg**
1 tablespoon parsley	**15 ml**
1 teaspoon minced garlic	**5 ml**
2 eggs	
Dash of nutmeg	
4 tablespoons plain breadcrumbs	**60 ml**
1 tablespoon grated parmigiano cheese	**15 ml**
2 tablespoons olive oil	**30 ml**

- Preheat oven to 400° (204°).
- Wash zucchini and cut off ends. Remove as much of pulp as possible with teaspoon and set aside.
- Wash, peel and cube potatoes. Set aside.
- In large mixing bowl, combine ground beef, parsley, garlic, eggs, nutmeg, salt and pepper to taste, breadcrumbs and parmigiano cheese. Use hands to mix thoroughly until all ingredients blend.
- Scoop mixture into zucchini. In 9 x 13-inch (23 x 33 cm) dish, add olive oil. Place stuffed zucchini and cubed potatoes in dish. Place dish in oven and bake about 1 to 1½ hours.

Serves 6.

Insalata di Pollo
(Chicken Salad)

This is great for a Saturday summer lunch. It can be easily prepared with leftover chicken. Insalata di Pollo can be enjoyed on sandwiches, crackers or for the more waist conscious just on its own.

4 boneless chicken breasts
8 baby carrots
½ cup mayonnaise   **120 ml**
Lettuce
Cherry tomatoes

- Sauté or broil chicken breasts. Cut into small cubes or thin strips.
- Steam carrots until tender but firm. Drain carrots, cool and slice.
- In bowl, combine chicken, carrots, mayonnaise, and salt and pepper to taste. Stir to mix well. Place in refrigerator to chill.
- When ready to serve, garnish platter with bed of lettuce. Place chicken salad on top of lettuce and garnish with cherry tomatoes.

Serves 4.

Petti di Pollo al Burro e Salvia
(Chicken Breasts With Butter and Sage)

This is a great, fast and delicious way to make chicken breasts. You will be amazed at how juicy and flavorful this dish is. The wonderful aroma of sage will surely interest everyone in the family.

4 chicken breasts, tenderized	
Flour	
4 tablespoons butter	**60 ml**
1 tablespoon olive oil	**15 ml**
1 tablespoon finely chopped onion	**15 ml**
¼ cup white wine	**60 ml**
6 leaves fresh sage	
1 lemon, sliced into wedges	

- Dredge tenderized chicken in flour and coat well on both sides.
- In skillet, combine butter, olive oil and onions and cook over medium to low heat.
- When onions are translucent, add chicken, brown on both sides and turn occasionally.
- Add wine, salt and pepper to taste and sage. Cook chicken thoroughly until juices are no longer pink.
- Place chicken on serving platter and garnish with lemon wedges.

Serves 4.

Pollo con Peperoni
(Chicken with Peppers)

This hearty and robust Roman dish is yet another great variation to preparing chicken. The light sauce created when cooking this dish is a true-bred attraction. Try it and see!

1 whole chicken	
4 small red, yellow or green peppers	
5 tablespoons olive oil	**75 ml**
½ cup finely chopped onion	**120 ml**
2 cloves garlic, peeled, crushed	
1 teaspoon crushed red pepper	**5 ml**
¾ cup white wine	**180 ml**
1 cube beef, chicken or vegetable bouillon	
1 (14 ounce) can crushed tomatoes	**396 g**
2 tablespoons fresh parsley	**30 ml**

- Wash chicken thoroughly and cut into serving-size pieces. Wash peppers, remove seeds and cut into strips. Set aside.

- In large pot, combine olive oil, onions, garlic and crushed red pepper. Cook over medium heat for 1 minute. Add chicken, brown on all sides for about 10 minutes and turn occasionally.

- Add wine and bouillon and cook until bouillon dissolves. Add peppers and stir to mix well. Cook for another 3 to 4 minutes. Stir in tomatoes and salt to taste.

- Turn heat to low, cover tightly and cook until peppers are soft and chicken cooks thoroughly, about 30 minutes.

- Remove from heat, stir in parsley and place on serving platter.

Serves 4.

Tip: If you don't want to cut up a chicken, just buy the chicken pieces you like.

Petti di Tacchino alla Fiorentina
(Turkey Breasts with Olives and Tomatoes)

This recipe will give you a whole new perspective on turkey. Dishes from the region of Florence are simple and plentiful. The variety and combination of flavors make this dish an absolute favorite.

5 tablespoons olive oil	**45 ml**
1 clove garlic, peeled, crushed	
4 turkey breasts, pounded	
¾ cup white wine	**180 ml**
4 Roma tomatoes, seeded, cut into strips	
1 cup pitted Kalamata olives	**240 ml**
8 leaves fresh basil, chopped	

- Heat olive oil and garlic over medium heat in skillet. Cook until garlic is just about golden.
- Add turkey breasts, salt and pepper to taste and sauté until turkey browns on all sides.
- Add wine and continue to cook about 5 minutes. Add tomatoes and olives and cook until turkey cooks thoroughly. Add basil and stir to mix well. Serve hot.

Serves 4.

Sformato di Patate
(Mashed Potato Casserole)

This is one of those dishes that seems elaborate, yet it's very easy to make. There are many ingredients, but all are readily available. We normally eat it hot and leftovers are even better the next day…hot or cold!

6 large Yukon or russett potatoes	
2 cups shredded mozzarella cheese	**480 ml**
2 tablespoons grated parmigiano cheese	**30 ml**
4-5 slices ham, diced	
3 eggs	
1 cup plus 3 tablespoons **breadcrumbs, divided**	**240 ml; 45 ml**
Dash of nutmeg	

- Preheat oven to 375° (190°C).
- Wash and peel potatoes. Cut into cubes and boil until tender enough to mash.
- Drain potatoes and place in large bowl. Mash potatoes with fork.
- Add mozzarella cheese, parmigiano cheese, diced ham, eggs, 1 cup (240 ml) breadcrumbs, salt and pepper to taste and nutmeg.
- Mix until ingredients blend well.
- Spray oven-safe dish with non-stick spray. Pour potato mixture in dish, sprinkle top with 3 tablespoons (45 ml) breadcrumbs and bake about 45 minutes or until golden brown.
- Remove from oven and let stand for several minutes. Serve hot.

Serves 4 to 6.

Filetto al Pepe
(Filet Mignon in Pepper Sauce)

You can put all sorts of commercial sauces and marinades on filet or steak, but they are not really popular in Italy. This incredibly simple yet superbly fancy recipe shows you why.

4 tablespoons whole peppercorn, divided	**60 ml**
4 filet mignon	
3 tablespoons butter	**45 ml**
4 tablespoons brandy	**60 ml**
½ cup heavy whipping cream	**120 ml**

- Grind peppercorns. Coat filets on both sides with 2 table-spoons (30 ml) ground peppercorns.
- Melt butter in large skillet. Add filets and brown over medium heat for 3 minutes on each side. Add salt to taste. Remove from skillet and set aside.
- In same skillet, add brandy, remainder of peppercorns and heavy whipping cream. Allow sauce to cook and thicken for about 1 minute.
- Place filets back in pan and continue to cook on both sides until meat cooks to your taste. Serve immediately.

Serves 4.

Melanzane alla Parmigiana
(Eggplant Parmesan)

This dish is one of our family's favorite and one of the greatest Neapolitan creations. Even those who ordinarily don't care for eggplant will love this saucy, cheesy combination. It is perfect to prepare ahead of time and refrigerate. It heats up beautifully even a couple of days later.

Sugo di Pomodoro Semplice: (Basic Red Sauce)

2 (28 ounce) cans whole, peeled or crushed tomatoes	2 (794 g)
3 tablespoons olive oil	45 ml
2 garlic cloves, peeled, minced	
1 teaspoon crushed red pepper	5 ml
4 leaves fresh basil	

- Blend tomatoes until smooth. In one large pot, add olive oil and garlic. Sauté garlic until just about golden.
- Add tomatoes, 2 teaspoons (10 ml) salt, crushed red pepper and basil leaves. Reduce heat to low and simmer for about 1½ hours.

Pastella: (Batter):

1 egg	
1 cup flour	240 ml
½ cup beer or sparkling mineral water	120 ml

- In separate bowl, combine egg, flour, beer or sparkling mineral water, salt and pepper to taste. Mix until smooth.

(Continued on next page.)

(*Continued*)

Melanzane alla Parmigiana:

Sugo di Pomodoro Semplice (page 80)
2 large eggplants
Pastella (page 80)
Olive oil
4-6 cups shredded mozzarella cheese   .9-1.5 ml
1 cup grated parmigiano cheese   240 ml

- Make Sugo di Pomodoro Semplice on page 80.
- Wash eggplant and cut into ¼-inch (.6 cm) slices. Sprinkle with salt and set aside.
- Make Pastella (Batter) recipe listed on page 80.
- Pat eggplant slices dry with paper towel. Place eggplant slices in egg-flour batter and toss to coat both sides.
- In large frying pan, heat oil on medium heat. Add 1 single layer of eggplant. Cover and cook over low to medium heat until light brown and soft.
- Remove cover and turn eggplant to cook on other side. Remove from pan, set aside and drain on paper towels.
- Coat sides and bottom of oven-safe dish with non-stick spray. Spread 1 layer of sauce on bottom. Alternate layers of eggplant, sauce, mozzarella and parmigiano.
- Repeat until all ingredients are used. Bake in oven about 30 minutes. Serve hot.

Serves 6.

Melanzane al Forno
(Baked Eggplant)

This is a great shortcut to Melanzane alla Parmigiana. The preparation is shorter, but the taste is no less than outstanding.

1 large eggplant, sliced	
Olive oil	
3 tablespoons dried oregano	**45 ml**
1 (28 ounce) can whole peeled or	
crushed tomatoes	**794 g**
1½ cups shredded mozzarella cheese	**360 ml**

- Preheat oven to 400° (204° C).
- Cut eggplant into ¼-inch (.6 cm) slices. In flat skillet, cook eggplant over medium heat about 1 minute on each side to remove excess liquid.
- Remove from skillet, place on baking sheet and brush with olive oil. Sprinkle salt and pepper to taste and dried oregano.
- Blend tomatoes in blender or food processor. Add tomato puree on each slice and top with mozzarella cheese.
- Bake until eggplant is tender and cheese bubbles, about 30 minutes. Serve hot.

Serves 4 to 6.

Scaloppine
(Breaded Veal Cutlets)

Scaloppine is an Italian term describing a thin scallop of meat. They are also known as veal cutlets.

4 veal cutlets	
Flour	
2 tablespoons olive oil	**30 ml**
½ cup white wine	**120 ml**
4 leaves fresh sage	
2 bay leaves	
2 tablespoons lemon juice	**30 ml**
1 lemon, sliced into wedges	

- Dredge veal in flour to cover both sides well.
- In large skillet, heat olive oil over medium heat. Place veal or (pounded chicken breasts) in skillet and sauté.
- Add white wine, salt and pepper to taste, sage, bay leaves and lemon juice. Cook until golden brown on both sides. Remove from pan and drain on paper towels.
- Serve with lemon wedges. Squeeze lemons over top of cutlets as desired.

Serves 4.

Fresh herbs provide a more authentic flavor to dishes in this cookbook, but dried herbs may be substituted in any of our recipes. As a general rule, dried herbs are more potent. If you are using dried herbs, you will want to reduce the required amount by half.

Involtini
(Scaloppine Wrap)

The word "involtini" means "small bundles". This traditional Italian dish is stuffed with delicious vegetables and herbs. Some regions of Italy include cheese in their stuffing. Our recipe does not, but with or without cheese, these are "bundles" of great taste!

¼ pound pancetta, sliced very thin, chopped	**114 g**
⅓ cup finely chopped onion	**80 ml**
⅓ cup finely chopped celery	**80 ml**
⅓ cup finely chopped carrots	**80 ml**
4 leaves fresh sage, chopped	
8 veal fillets, sliced very thin by butcher	
3 tablespoons olive oil	**45 ml**
1 cup white wine	**240 ml**
1 cube vegetable bouillon	

- Combine pancetta, vegetables and sage in medium bowl and mix.
- On each slice of veal, sprinkle salt and pepper to taste. Add layer of pancetta mixture on each slice of veal.
- Roll each slice and close securely with toothpicks. (Be sure toothpicks keep all vegetables contained.)
- In large saucepan, heat olive oil and any remaining chopped vegetables on low to medium heat about 5 minutes.
- Place Involtini in pan and brown on all sides. Add white wine. Allow wine to cook out for a few minutes and add vegetable bouillon and 1 cup (240 ml) water.
- Cover and cook over low heat for 45 minutes. Check liquid in pan. If it reduces too much, add up to ½ cup (120 ml) water. Cook until meat appears nice and brown. Serve hot.

Serves 4.

Saltimbocca alla Romana
(Veal Wraps)

This is one of the most classic Roman dishes you will ever try. The literal translation of the name is "hop in the mouth" and it's truly fitting for this dish. The delicious blend of sage and prociutto flavors will entice you to keep eating!

10 small veal fillets, thinly sliced	
10 slices prosciutto	
10 leaves fresh sage	
¼ cup (½ stick) butter	**60 ml**
¼ onion, finely chopped	
¾ cup beef, chicken or vegetable stock, warmed	**180 ml**

- On each slice of veal, lay 1 slice prosciutto and 1 sage leaf. Sprinkle with salt and pepper to taste. Roll and secure with toothpicks.
- Melt butter in skillet. Add onions and cook until they are translucent. Add veal and sauté for approximately 5 to 8 minutes. Turn to brown on all sides.
- Add broth and continue cooking about 3 more minutes.
- Remove from heat. Place veal on serving platter. Serve hot with remaining juices as gravy.

Serves 4.

Salvia (Sage) is another versatile and widely used herb that is intensely fragrant. It is a wonderful addition to recipes with pork or veal. Once cooked, its aroma is absolutely delightful.

Polpette
(Meatballs)

This is a great dish to put together when you are short on time. Unlike American meatballs, Italian polpette are not meant to be eaten with pasta. They want and deserve all the attention to themselves. These are best paired with one of our great vegetable side dishes.

2 slices white sandwich bread	
1 cup milk	**240 ml**
½ pound ground pork	**114 g**
½ pound ground beef	**114 g**
1 egg	
2 teaspoons minced garlic	**10 ml**
1 tablespoon finely chopped fresh parsley	**15 ml**
Dash of nutmeg	
2 tablespoons grated parmigiano cheese	**30 ml**
Breadcrumbs	
Cooking oil	
1 small lemon, cut into wedges, optional	

- Soak sandwich bread in milk. Combine ground pork, ground beef, egg, garlic, parsley, salt and pepper to taste, nutmeg, parmigiano cheese and milk-soaked bread. Mix well.
- Make meatballs small enough to fit in palm of your hand. Roll each ball into plate with breadcrumbs. Breadcrumbs should coat meatballs well.
- In large, deep skillet, heat cooking oil over medium heat. Place meatballs in skillet and be sure meatballs are not touching or on top of one another.
- Turn meatballs occasionally. If meatballs are cooking too quickly, reduce heat.
- Cook until brown, about 20 minutes. Remove with slotted spoon and drain on paper towel. Serve with lemon wedges, if desired.

Serves 4 to 6.

Tip: Pork and ground beef can be used as a combination or separately.

Polpette di Verdura
(Vegetarian Meatballs)

My mother first made these for me and now I make them for my family all the time! They are delicious and always taste great. They also re-heat very well.

1 cup cubed eggplant	**240 ml**
½ cup sliced baby carrots	**120 ml**
½ cup sliced zucchini	**120 ml**
1 tablespoon olive oil	**15 ml**
2 eggs	
2 tablespoons grated parmigiano cheese	**30 ml**
1 tablespoon finely chopped fresh parsley	**15 ml**
¼ cup plain breadcrumbs	**60 ml**
1 clove garlic, peeled, minced	
Flour	
Breadcrumbs	
Olive oil	

- Steam zucchini in boiling water for 5 minutes. Remove zucchini and set aside. Add carrots to same boiling water and steam for 20 minutes. Drain and set aside.
- In medium skillet, combine olive oil and eggplant. Sauté about 5 minutes. Remove from heat and set aside.
- In blender or food processor, purée vegetables and set aside. In large bowl, combine eggs, parmigiano, parsley, breadcrumbs, garlic, salt and pepper to taste. Stir to mix well. Add puréed vegetables. Stir to mix well.
- Form vegetarian meatballs small enough to fit in palm of hand. Roll each ball into bowl of flour and then plate with breadcrumbs. Coat meatballs well.
- In large, deep skillet, heat cooking oil over medium heat. Place meatballs in skillet and be sure meatballs are not touching or on top of one another.
- Turn meatballs occasionally. If meatballs are cooking too quickly, reduce heat.
- Cook about 10 to 12 minutes. Remove with slotted spoon to paper towel to drain.

Serves 4.

Braciole di Maiale
(Seared Pork Chops)

This extremely simple dish will be a delightful surprise at the table. It gives you tender, juicy chops that are great for just a weeknight family dinner or an evening with company.

2½ **tablespoons olive oil**	**37 ml**
2 **garlic cloves, peeled, crushed**	
4 **boneless pork chops**	
2 **sprigs fresh rosemary**	
2 **bay leaves**	
2 **tablespoons lemon juice**	**30 ml**
⅓ **cup white wine**	**80 ml**

- Heat oil on medium heat in large skillet. Add garlic and cook until just about golden.
- Place pork chops in skillet and add salt and pepper to taste, rosemary and bay leaves. Brown both sides of meat and add lemon juice and white wine.
- Continue to cook over medium heat. Be sure to turn chops from time to time. Pork chops are done when outside is light brown. Be sure pork chops cook thoroughly.

Serves 4.

Braciole alle Olive Verdi
(Savory Olive Pork Chops)

Green olives work quite well with pork chops. If you are looking for a main course dish you can serve up in about 30 minutes, then these pork chops are the way to go.

4 boneless pork chops	
Flour	
3 tablespoons olive oil	**45 ml**
2 fresh bay leaves	
1 teaspoon crushed red pepper	**5 ml**
½ cup white wine	**120 ml**
¼ cup chopped green olives	**60 ml**

- With meat mallet, tenderize pork chops. Dredge in flour and coat well on both sides.
- In skillet over medium heat, combine olive oil, bay leaves and crushed red pepper.
- Add pork chops and brown about 7 minutes on each side. Add white wine and cook until wine evaporates. Add olives and cook about 2 more minutes. Serve hot.

Serves 4.

Foglie di Alloro (Bay Leaves) are leaves from the laurel trees of Ancient Greece and add savory flavor to soups, stews and meat sauces.

Spiedini alla Griglia
Grilled Italian-Style Shish-Kabobs

This is a tantalizing version of shish-kabobs. The marinade will make the meat tender and will keep it from drying out. These are great for informal get-togethers and offer a creative alternative to traditional barbecue.

Marinade:

3 tablespoons olive oil	45 ml
1 garlic clove, peeled	
2 sprigs fresh rosemary	
2 bay leaves	
1 teaspoon dried oregano	5 ml
1 tablespoon lemon juice	15 ml

- In large bowl, combine olive oil, garlic, rosemary, bay leaves, oregano, salt and pepper to taste and lemon juice. Stir to mix well.
- Place chicken, pork and sausage in olive oil mixture. Coat meat well, cover and place in refrigerator for up to 4 hours.
- Assemble kebobs, *Spiedini*, alternating meats and vegetables on wooden or metal skewer. Grill until meat cooks thoroughly. Serve hot.

Spiedini alla Griglia:

2 large chicken breasts, cut into bite-size pieces	
2 boneless pork chops, cut into bite-size pieces	
3 links sausage, cut into bite-size pieces	
2 red, green or yellow peppers	
1 large onion	
1 cup fresh mushrooms	240 ml
3 Roma tomatoes	

Serves 6.

Arrosto di Maiale con Erbe e Aglio
(Pork Roast with Herbs and Garlic)

The secret to a great roast is the size of the piece of meat as well as the method of cooking. This pork tenderloin is an elegant and surprisingly fast meal. Our blend of herbs will make this dish memorable.

1 pork tenderloin
1 garlic clove, peeled

Marinade:
3 tablespoons olive oil	**45 ml**
2 sprigs fresh rosemary	
4 leaves sage	
1 sprig thyme	
2 bay leaves	
1 tablespoon lemon juice	**15 ml**

- Lay pork tenderloin flat and rub with garlic clove.
- In large bowl, combine olive oil, garlic, rosemary, sage, thyme, bay leaves, salt and pepper to taste and lemon juice. Stir to mix well.
- Add pork tenderloin and marinate about 2 hours in refrigerator.
- Preheat oven to 400° (204° C).
- Place pork with marinade in oven-safe dish and cook for 1 hour or until it cooks thoroughly.
- Remove from oven and serve on platter with cooked marinade drizzled over pork tenderloin or served from gravy boat.

Serves 4 to 6.

Polpettone di Tacchino
(Turkey Meatloaf)

This is a perfect recipe to prepare ahead of time. We love to use turkey in several of our dishes because it's lean and deliciously good when the right herbs and spices blend.

2 slices white sandwich bread	
1 cup milk	**240 ml**
1 pound ground turkey	**.5 kg**
1 egg	
1-2 tablespoons plain breadcrumbs	**30 ml**
1 tablespoon fresh parsley	**15 ml**
2 teaspoons minced garlic	**10 ml**
1 tablespoon grated parmigiano cheese	**15 ml**
Dash of nutmeg	
Olive oil	
8-10 whole baby carrots	
¼ cup chopped onion	**60 ml**
1 cube vegetable bouillon	
¼ cup white wine	**60 ml**

- Soak 2 slices sandwich bread in bowl of milk.
- In large bowl, combine ground turkey, egg, breadcrumbs, parsley, garlic, parmigiano cheese, salt and pepper to taste, nutmeg and milk-soaked bread. Mix well until all ingredients blend well. Form mixture into meatloaf.
- In wide pot, heat oil, onions and carrots on medium heat. Cook until onions are translucent. Add meatloaf and brown on all sides.
- Add bouillon and white wine. Reduce heat, cover and simmer 1 to 1½ hours. Turn often to cook on all sides. Serve hot.

Serves 4.

Tip: This recipe may be used to make meatballs with turkey instead of ground beef.

Salsicce con Broccoletti
(Sausage with Broccoletti)

This recipe works the best when you use Italian sausage. Serve this delicacy with some focaccia and we guarantee that there will be no leftovers to put in the fridge.

1 pound broccoletti	**. 5 kg**
1 pound Italian-style sausage	**. 5 kg**
2 tablespoons olive oil	**30 ml**
2 garlic cloves, peeled, minced	
1 teaspoon crushed red pepper	**5 ml**
¼ cup white wine	**60 ml**

- Steam broccoletti about 5 minutes. Drain and set aside.
- Combine olive oil, garlic and crushed red pepper in skillet and cook over medium heat until garlic is just about golden.
- Add sausage and white wine and cook until sausage browns on all sides. Add broccoletti and a little salt. Stir to mix well.
- Reduce heat to low and continue cooking about 10 minutes. Serve hot.

Serves 4.

Rolle
(Stuffed Flank Steak)

This is a great way to transform an inexpensive cut of meat into an incredible feast. The secret is to tenderize the meat before cooking. It pairs very well with our sautéed asparagus.

2 eggs, hard-boiled	
4-6 baby carrots, steamed, sliced	
1½ pounds flank steak	**.7 kg**
2 slices baked ham	
½ cup olive oil	**120 ml**
2 tablespoons butter	**30 ml**
2 sprigs fresh rosemary	
¼ cup finely chopped onion	**60 ml**
2 garlic cloves, peeled, crushed	
½ cup vegetable stock	**120 ml**
¼ cup white wine	**60 ml**

- Peel eggs and chill in refrigerator. When cool, slice and set aside.
- Steam carrots until tender, but firm. Drain and set aside.
- Use meat mallet to tenderize steak on both sides. Sprinkle salt and pepper to taste.
- Lay slices of ham, carrots and eggs on flank steak. Roll flank steak and secure with twine.
- In semi-deep pot, combine olive oil, butter, garlic, rosemary and onion and cook over medium heat. Add flank steak and brown on all sides.
- When meat browns on all sides, add vegetable stock and wine. Reduce heat and cook about 1½ to 2 hours.
- Remove twine prior to slicing and serving.

Serves 4.

Spezzatino con Patate
(Beef Stew with Potatoes)

This is not your everyday "beef stew". This hearty, robust dish is particularly enjoyable on a cold winter day. You will love the almost creamy consistency of the potatoes.

4 medium russett potatoes	
1 cube vegetable bouillon	
2 tablespoons olive oil	**30 ml**
½ cup chopped white onion	**120 ml**
8 whole baby carrots	
½ rib celery	
1 pound beef stew meat	**. 5 kg**
¼ cup white wine	**60 ml**
1 sprig fresh rosemary	

- Peel potatoes and cut into large pieces and set aside.
- Fill glass measuring cup with 1 cup (240 ml) water and add vegetable bouillon. Place in microwave and cook on HIGH about 1 minute or until bouillon dissolves. Remove from microwave and set aside.
- In large pot, combine olive oil, onions, carrots and celery. Sauté until onions are translucent. Add stew meat, mix well and cook until it browns.
- Add wine and simmer for 3 to 4 minutes.
- Add potatoes and vegetable stock. Stir to mix well and add rosemary. Cover, simmer on low heat about 1 hour or until potatoes are tender and stir occasionally.
- Remove from heat, remove celery stalk and serve hot.

Serves 4 to 6.

Fettine alla Pizzaiola
(Pizzaiola Meat)

No self-respecting Italian cook would be complete without pizzaiola meat. This dish is so humble and simple we are really not sure who invented it or how it got its name, but it is superb!

1 pound veal, beef rump or beef chuck roast, thinly sliced	.5 kg
2 tablespoons olive oil	30 ml
2 garlic cloves, peeled, crushed	
1 (14 ounce) can whole peeled or crushed tomatoes, blended	396 g
2-3 teaspoons dried oregano	10-15 ml
1 teaspoon crushed red pepper	5 ml

- With sharp knife, cut edges of meat to prevent curling during cooking.
- In large frying pan, heat olive oil and garlic on medium heat. Add tomatoes, oregano, salt to taste and crushed red pepper. Cook over medium heat about 10 to 15 minutes. Add ¼ cup (60 ml) water and meat. Cook until meat is thoroughly done. Serve hot.

Serves 4 to 6.

Origano (Oregano) is best known as the "pizza herb" because of the zest it adds to many pizza recipes. Oregano adds a very assertive flavor to just about any Italian dish, especially ones with red meat, roasted chicken, tomato-based sauces and fish.

Fettine Panate
(Breaded Veal)

This is a favorite in the region of Milan where it is actually called Cotoletta alla Milanese, *which literally translates into cutlet Milanese-style. We gave it a slightly different name, but the taste is just as delicious.*

2 eggs
8 veal fillets, thinly sliced
Plain breadcrumbs
Cooking oil
1 lemon, cut into wedges

- Beat eggs in large, shallow bowl. Add salt and pepper to taste. Coat meat on both sides with egg mixture.
- Place meat in breadcrumbs and coat on both sides.
- Pour cooking oil in skillet and heat on high. When oil is hot, add meat and reduce heat to medium.
- Turn frequently and cook until golden brown. Remove meat and place on paper towel to remove excess oil.
- Arrange on platter and garnish with lemon wedges. Serve hot.

Serves 6.

Cozze al Vino Bianco
(Steamed Mussels in White Wine)

This is a nice centerpiece for a hearty, fish-based meal. Be prepared to consume huge quantities of bread, because nothing absorbs the great sauce better. The sauce makes the dish and a freshly baked focaccia or a nice, crusty bread is perfect with it.

1½ **pounds fresh mussels in shells**	**.7 kg**
3 **tablespoons olive oil**	**45 ml**
2 **garlic cloves, peeled, crushed**	
1½ **teaspoons crushed red pepper**	**7 ml**
1½ **cups white wine**	**360 ml**
¼ **cup finely chopped fresh parsley**	**60 ml**

- Wash mussels in running water. In large skillet, heat olive oil, garlic and crushed red pepper over medium heat. When oil is hot, add mussels.

- Cover, reduce heat and cook for 5 minutes. Add white wine, parsley and salt to taste. Continue to cook until all shells are open.

Serves 4 to 6.

Tip: Discard mussel if shell does not open.

Gamberoni in Padella
(Sautéed Jumbo Shrimp)

This is not your usual shrimp dish, but one that is quite literally "finger-licking good!" This fast, easy, heart-healthy dish will really astonish your taste buds!

1½ pounds jumbo shrimp, cleaned, veined with shell	**680 g**
3 tablespoons olive oil	**45 ml**
2 garlic cloves, peeled, crushed	
1½ teaspoons crushed red pepper	**7 ml**
½ cup crushed tomatoes, optional	**120 ml**

- Wash shrimp and set aside.
- In frying pan, combine olive oil, garlic, salt to taste, crushed red pepper and tomatoes, if desired.
- Sauté until garlic is just about golden. Add shrimp, reduce heat and cook until shrimp turn pink. Place shrimp in serving dish and drizzle remaining oil mixture over them. Serve hot.

Serves 4 to 6.

Herbs add depth to flavor and provide instant zest to all Italian recipes. Herbs can be classified as either hardy or tender. Herbs such as bay leaves, oregano, sage and rosemary are considered hardy herbs. They are tougher and generally are added to the recipe toward the beginning of the cooking process. Herbs such as parsley and basil are considered tender herbs because they are lighter. These herbs are typically added toward the end of cooking.

Baccalá Frítto
(Fried Cod)

Frying cod is simplicity in itself. The key is the batter. Follow our directions closely and you will be amazed at how wonderful this dish is. It's crunchy on the outside and soft and tender on the inside. Even non-fish lovers will love this dish!

Cooking oil
Pastella (recipe below)
4 fresh or frozen cod fillets
Lemon, sliced into wedges

Pastella: (Batter)

1 egg, beaten	
1 cup flour	**240 ml**
½ cup beer or sparkling mineral water	**120 ml**

- Heat oil in skillet on high heat.
- Mix egg, flour, beer or mineral water, salt and pepper to taste. Dip cod into batter, coat and place in oil. Reduce heat to low. Sprinkle cod pieces with a little salt and pepper.
- Cook until golden brown. Remove and place on paper towel to remove excess oil.
- Serve with lemon wedges.

Serves 4.

Tip: Fresh cod always tastes a little better.

Baccalá al Forno
(Baked Cod)

Since childhood, I have always associated this dish with warmth and security. The best way I know to describe this wonderful dish is to call it "my comfort food".

2 tablespoons olive oil	**30 ml**
4 fresh or frozen cod fillets	
1½ cups crushed tomatoes	**360 ml**
¼ cup chopped onion	**60 ml**
⅓ cup pitted black olives, halved	**80 ml**
1½ teaspoons oregano	**7 ml**

- Preheat oven to 375° (190° C).
- In oven-safe dish, combine olive oil, cod, tomatoes, onion, olives, salt and pepper to taste and oregano.
- Bake in oven about 20 to 25 minutes. Turn occasionally to cook evenly on all sides.

Serves 4.

It's no secret that **tomatoes** are a critical part of Italian cooking. They are healthy and can be turned into many wonderful sauces. There are many varieties to choose from including whole, crushed and diced. We recommend that you keep your shelves well stocked with plenty of canned tomatoes.

Pesce Bianco con Capperi
(Seared Seabass with Capers)

This is one of the most delicate fish dishes that you will ever try. It's quite an impressive dish considering how easy it is. It is delicious, yet subtle and sure to impress any dinner guest.

4 fillets sea bass	
Flour	
⅓ cup (⅔ stick) butter, divided	**80 ml**
2 tablespoons flour	**30 ml**
¼ cup capers	**60 ml**
2 tablespoons lemon juice	**30 ml**
1 cup white wine	**240 ml**

- Preheat oven to 350° (176° C).
- In large bowl, dredge fillets in flour and coat well on both sides.
- In skillet over medium heat, melt ¼ cup (60 ml) butter. Add coated fillets and brown on both sides. Do not overcook sea bass because it will continue to cook in oven.
- Remove sea bass from skillet and place in oven-safe dish coated with non-stick spray. Do not discard pan juices. Place in oven and bake about 20 minutes.
- In skillet, melt remaining butter. Add 2 tablespoons (30 ml) flour and stir continuously.
- Add capers, lemon juice and white wine. Cook on low heat for about 5 minutes.
- Remove sea bass from oven. Arrange sea bass on serving platter and pour pan juices over it. Serve hot.

Serves 4.

Sogliola alla Mugnaia
(Sautéed Dover Sole)

This is one of the finest ways to prepare sole. It is important to remember that sole is a very tender fish and cooks rather fast. Enjoy this delicate dish with Fagiolini con Patate (page 110).

Flour	
4 fillets Dover sole	
¼ cup (4 tablespoons) butter	**60 ml**
¼ cup white wine	**60 ml**
Lemon juice	
4 leaves fresh sage, chopped	
1 lemon, cut into wedges	

- In large bowl, dredge fillets in flour and coat well on both sides.
- Melt butter in skillet over medium heat. Add fillets and brown on both sides.
- Add wine, lemon juice, sage, salt and pepper to taste.
- Remove from skillet to serving platter and garnish with lemon wedges.

Serves 4.

Tip: Because sole is a very tender fish, it cooks very fast. Depending on the thickness, cooking time will likely be no longer than 7 minutes.

Sogliola al Forno
(Oven-Baked Dover Sole)

This is a great variation for Dover sole. It is a lighter version of Sauteed Dover Sole, but the taste is not compromised.

3 cups milk	**710 ml**
6 fillets Dover sole	
3 tablespoons olive oil	**45 ml**

- Preheat oven to 375° (190° C).
- In large bowl, combine milk and a little salt. Add fillets and coat well on both sides.
- In oven-safe dish, coat bottom with olive oil and add fillets. Place dish in oven, cook about 15 to 20 minutes and turn once.

Serves 6.

Filetti di Salmone in Padella
(Sautéed Salmon Fillets)

This quick-and-easy recipe makes the salmon tender and juicy. It pairs very well with our "Spinaci con Limone" (page 117).

3 tablespoons butter	**45 ml**
¼ cup chopped onion	**60 ml**
4 fresh salmon fillets	
1 teaspoon crushed red pepper	**5 ml**
2 sprigs fresh thyme	
2 tablespoons lemon juice	**30 ml**
⅓ cup white wine	**80 ml**

- Add butter and onion to skillet and sauté until onions are translucent.
- Add salmon, salt to taste, crushed red pepper and thyme and cook over low to medium heat. Brown on both sides.
- Add lemon juice and wine and continue to cook until salmon turns pink, about 15 to 20 minutes. Serve hot.

Serves 4.

Salmone con Peperoni
(Salmon with Peppers)

This scrumptious and beautiful entrée combines the flavor of salmon fillets with the sweet flavor of cooked peppers. The combination is tantalizing to say the least!

2 tablespoons olive oil	**30 ml**
¼ cup finely chopped onion	**60 ml**
1 red bell pepper, sliced	
1 green bell pepper, sliced	
1 cube vegetable bouillon	
4 salmon fillets, fresh or frozen	

- Combine olive oil, onion and peppers in skillet. Sauté about 10 minutes.
- Add vegetable bouillon and stir until it dissolves.
- Add salmon fillets and sprinkle with salt and pepper to taste. Cover, simmer on low heat about 15 to 20 minutes and turn occasionally.

Serves 4.

Spiedini di Mare
(Seafood Skewers)

This is a great light, healthy and simple yet impressive entree. For those who are watching the waistline, simply skip the butter sauce and replace with fresh lemon wedges.

16 large shrimp, cleaned, veined	
16 large scallops	
2 (8 ounce) tuna fish fillet	**2 (227 g)**
6 tablespoons olive oil	**90 ml**
1½ cups plain breadcrumbs	**360 ml**
1 cup lemon juice	**240 ml**
1 cup chicken broth	**240 ml**
1 cup white wine	**240 ml**
3 tablespoons flour	**45 ml**
5 tablespoons butter, softened	**75 ml**
½ cup chopped fresh parsley	**120 ml**

- Cut fish into 2-inch (5 cm) chunks. Place 2 shrimps, 2 scallops and 2 pieces fish on each skewer in alternating pattern. Brush with oil and carefully roll in breadcrumbs.

- In saucepan, heat lemon juice, chicken broth and wine over medium-low heat. In a medium bowl, mix flour into softened butter.

- Whisk flour mixture into lemon mixture a little at a time. Continue to whisk until it reaches desired consistency. Reduce heat to low while seafood cooks on grill.

- Grill skewers over high heat, 3 minutes on each side or until done. When seafood is done, stir parsley into mixture and remove from heat. Place seafood skewers on platter and drizzle sauce over top. Serve hot.

Serves 4.

Verdure e Contorni
Vegetables
and Side Dishes

*— Cose buone e genuine per
accompagnare un pasto delizioso! —*

*— Genuinely good things
accompany a delicious meal! —*

Patate Arrosto
(Roasted Potatoes)

Everyone loves potatoes. Even people who don't like vegetables like potatoes! You will love everything about our deliciously yummy Patate Arrosto!

6-8 potatoes
4 tablespoons olive oil   **60 ml**
2 garlic cloves, peeled, crushed
3 sprigs rosemary

- Preheat oven to 350° (176° C).
- Wash and peel potatoes. Cut in half, then into quarters. Set potatoes aside.
- In oven-safe dish, add olive oil, garlic, potatoes, salt and pepper to taste and rosemary and mix.
- Place in oven, bake until golden brown, about 1½ hours, and stir occasionally. Cook longer for crunchier potatoes.

Serves 4 to 6.

Rosmarino (Rosemary) is a very aromatic herb and grows wild throughout Italy. It is because of this property that it is so widely used in many Mediterranean recipes. Most households in Italy actually keep a little pot of this wonderful herb on their balconies so that it's readily available to them for all their cooking needs. It adds bold flavor to many meat recipes.

Patate Affogate
(Drowned Potatoes)

This wonderful dish gets its name because the potatoes are completely covered with water during cooking, thus "drowned".

4-6 Yukon potatoes	
3 tablespoons olive oil	**45 ml**
2 garlic cloves, peeled, crushed	
1 tablespoon fresh parsley	**15 ml**

- Wash, peel and cut potatoes into cubes.
- Combine olive oil, garlic, potatoes, salt and pepper to taste in saucepan over medium heat.
- Add 1 cup (240 ml) water and cover tightly. Cook about 15 to 20 minutes. Stir potatoes occasionally, cover and continue to cook until potatoes are nice and tender.
- Remove from heat. Add parsley and stir to mix well. Serve hot.

Serves 4 to 6.

Tip: One head of cauliflower may be substituted for the potatoes.

Insalata di Fagiolini e Patate
(Green Bean and Potato Salad)

This salad is delicious served cold and it's perfect for hot, summer months.

3 medium potatoes	
½ pound fresh green beans	**227 g**
2-3 tablespoons olive oil	**30-45 ml**
1½ tablespoons red balsamic vinegar	**22 ml**
1 garlic clove, peeled, finely chopped	

- Wash, peel and cut potatoes in half. Boil potatoes about 30 minutes or until tender. Drain potatoes and cool for 30 minutes.
- While potatoes boil, wash green beans and remove ends. Steam green beans for 20 minutes or until tender. Drain and cool for 30 minutes.
- Cut potatoes into quarters. Place potatoes and green beans in medium bowl and add oil, vinegar, salt and pepper to taste and garlic. Stir to mix well.
- Place in refrigerator about 20 minutes. Serve chilled.

Serves 4 to 6.

Tip: Yukon potatoes are best for this recipe.

True **balsamic vinegar** comes from Modena in the northern part of Italy near the gulf of Genoa. It is made from the unfermented juice of white grapes that have a high sugar content. This juice is placed into wooden barrels with some older balsamic vinegar to begin the process of acetification. The vinegar is transferred to different wood barrels each year to obtain flavors of the different woods. Young vinegar is 3 to 5 years old, middle aged is 6 to 12 years old and very mature balsamic vinegar is 12 up to 150 years old.

Insalata di Riso
(Rice Salad)

Rice salad is truly a classic summer dish. You can vary this recipe greatly depending on different preferences and taste. We love this one with tuna because it's light and refreshing.

3 cups Arborio or basmati rice	**710 ml**
5 Roma tomatoes	
1 (6 ounce) can tuna, drained	**168 g**
1 tablespoon finely chopped parlsey	**15 ml**
2 lemons	
3 tablespoons olive oil	**45 ml**

- Cook rice according to package directions. Cut tomatoes into small cubes, drain and set aside.
- Drain tuna and fluff with fork.
- Drain rice and rinse under cold water.
- Pour rice in serving bowl. Add tomatoes, parsley, tuna, lemon juice, olive oil and salt to taste. Chill and serve.

Serves 4.

Tip: Mayonnaise may be substituted for lemon juice.

Balsamic vinegar is absolutely great for cooking and for marinating meats and poultry. The less expensive versions of balsamic vinegar have brown sugar or caramel added to mimic the sweetness of true balsamic vinegar. Since the taste is concentrated, a little bit goes a long way. Try to find a medium priced version for everyday cooking.

Bortlotti Conditi
(Dressed Butter Beans)

This is fast and a super easy way to create a wonderful side dish and it pairs well with any meat, poultry or fish.

1 (15 ounce) can butter beans	**425 g**
½ rib celery, chopped	
1 ½ tablespoons finely chopped onion	**22 ml**
1 ½ tablespoons olive oil	**22 ml**

- Drain beans and rinse. In a medium bowl, combine beans, celery, onion, olive oil, salt and pepper to taste.
- Stir to mix well. Serve cold or room temperature.

Serves 4.

Tip: For a hearty salad, drain 1 (6 ounce/168 g) can tuna and add ingredients. Serve with crackers.

Funghi in Padella
(Sautéed Mushrooms)

One secret to preparing great mushrooms is not to wash them too much. They absorb a lot of water that comes out during cooking.

1 pound mushrooms, sliced	**. 5 kg**
2 tablespoons olive oil	**30 ml**
1-2 cloves garlic, peeled, crushed	
1 teaspoon crushed red pepper	**5 ml**
1 ½ tablespoons chopped parsley,	**22 ml**

- Heat olive oil, garlic and crushed red pepper in skillet over medium heat.
- Add mushrooms, parsley and salt to taste. Cook until mushrooms are tender.

Serves 4 to 6.

Sformato di Zucchine e Pane
(Zucchini and Bread Crumble)

Zucchini has a mild flavor and sometimes needs to be given a little personality with the addition of spices and other ingredients. This recipe is full of personality with popular Italian cheeses and a crumbled bread topping.

1½ pounds zucchini	680 g
5 tablespoons olive oil, divided	75 ml
1 whole clove garlic, peeled	
2 cups shredded mozzarella cheese	480 ml
½ cup grated parmigiano cheese	120 ml
3 slices white bread, crust removed	
1 tablespoon chopped fresh basil	15 ml
1 tablespoon chopped fresh parsley	15 ml

- Preheat oven to 350° (176° C).
- Wash zucchini and cut ends off. Grate zucchini and dry thoroughly with paper towels.
- Combine 2 tablespoons (30 ml) olive oil and garlic in skillet. Add zucchini, stir to mix well and cook about 5 minutes. Remove and discard garlic clove.
- Butter oven-safe dish. Add 1 layer zucchini, 1 layer mozzarella and 1 layer parmigiano. Continue alternating layers, ending with mozzarella, until all ingredients are gone.
- Blend bread, basil and parsley in blender. Pour over top of layered zucchini mixture. Drizzle remaining olive oil over top. Bake in oven for 20 to 25 minutes. Serve hot.

Serves 4.

Broccolo Bianco con Parmigiano
(Cauliflower in Parmigiano Sauce)

There are a number of ways to sauce up cauliflower. This recipe uses a creamy parmigiano cheese sauce with the addition of some crushed red pepper just to kick things up a notch.

1 medium cauliflower	
¼ cup olive oil	**60 ml**
2 tablespoons flour	**30 ml**
½ cup grated parmigiano cheese	**120 ml**
½ teaspoon crushed red pepper	**2 ml**
¼ cup chopped fresh parsley	**60 ml**
Juice of fresh lemon	

- Clean and trim cauliflower. Cut into florets. Bring large pot of water with a little rock salt to boil.
- Place florets into water and cook about 5 to 7 minutes or until tender. Drain and set aside.
- Combine olive oil, flour, parmigiano and crushed red pepper in large skillet over medium heat. Stir well and cook about 3 minutes.
- Add cauliflower and mix so all florets are well coated. Cook for another 4 to 5 minutes.
- Add salt to taste and sprinkle with parsley. Squeeze lemon juice over top before serving. May be served hot or cold.

Serves 4.

Cauliflower most likely originated in Asia Minor, but it was used almost exclusively in Italy until the 16th century. It was then introduced to France and eventually other areas of Europe.

Peperoni Arrosto
(Roasted Bell Peppers)

This is one of our favorites. There are so many uses for roasted peppers. This is a fabulous side dish. Try them on bruschetta too or make a sandwich on some focaccia. Truly memorable!

4 red, green or yellow bell peppers	
2 tablespoons olive oil	**30 ml**
2 cloves garlic, peeled, crushed	
1 tablespoon chopped parsley	**15 ml**

- Preheat oven to 400° (204° C).
- Wash peppers, place on oven rack and cook about 30 minutes.
- Remove peppers from oven and cool for a few minutes.
- Peel and discard skin from peppers. Cut in half and remove seeds. Rinse under cool running water.
- Cut into strips and place in bowl. Add remainder of ingredients. Stir to mix well. Serve chilled.

Serves 4 to 6.

Spinaci in Padella
(Sautéed Spinach)

Spinach goes particularly well with fish or meat. This is a very popular vegetable throughout Italy. We prepare them in many different ways, all good and all delicious!

2 tablespoons olive oil	**30 ml**
1-2 cloves garlic, peeled, crushed	
1 teaspoon crushed red pepper	**5 ml**
2 pounds fresh spinach	**1 kg**

- Heat oil in medium skillet over moderate heat. Add garlic and crushed red pepper and cook on low to medium heat for 1 to 2 minutes until garlic is just about golden.
- Add spinach and sauté. Sprinkle with salt to taste.
- Mix thoroughly and continue to cook for 2 to 3 more minutes. Serve hot.

Serves 4 to 6.

If you want to pep up your pasta and add some heat, **crushed red pepper** is the spice for you. Crushed red pepper is made from dried, whole chili peppers that have been crushed or coarsely ground. It is a very popular spice and is commonly found on the tables at most pizza eateries. A little bit goes a long way, so it is best to start with a small amount, then add more if you dare.

Spinaci con Limone
(Steamed Spinach with Lemon)

Here is an excellent variation of this popular vegetable. The beauty of this dish is its simplicity. The delicate spinach leaves are steamed and coated with a refreshing lemon mixture to brighten the entire dish.

2 pounds fresh spinach	**1 kg**
2 tablespoons olive oil	**30 ml**
2 tablespoons lemon juice	**30 ml**

- Steam spinach about 10 minutes. Remove and drain. Set aside to cool for a few minutes.
- Cut spinach and combine with olive oil, salt and pepper to taste and lemon in serving bowl.
- Mix well and serve. Spinach may be served at room temperature or chilled. Enjoy!

Serves 4 to 6.

Tip: Zucchini may be used in place of spinach. Cut zucchini into slices and follow the same directions.

Zucchine al Pomodoro
(Zucchini with Tomatoes)

This remarkable dish has zucchini rounds sauteed in a simplified version of the classic red sauce. The recipe is a particular favorite of our children. They don't even realize they are eating vegetables.

4 small zucchini	
2 tablespoons olive oil	**30 ml**
¼ cup finely chopped onion	**60 ml**
¾ cup crushed tomatoes	**180 ml**
3 basil leaves	

- Wash and slice zucchini into ¼-inch (.6 cm) rounds and set aside.
- Combine olive oil, onions, tomatoes, salt and pepper to taste in skillet. Sauté about 15 minutes.
- Add zucchini and basil leaves. Stir to mix well. Continue to cook until zucchini are tender, about 10 to 15 minutes. Serve hot.

Serves 4.

Basilico (Basil) is truly an incredible herb that is quite fragrant and refreshing. It is considered a symbol of love to Italians. Basil is enjoyed for its rich and spicy, mildly peppery flavor with a trace of mint and clove. It is typically used in many tomato-based sauces, salads, and soups. It can easily be grown in a pot and placed on a windowsill indoors, but, it does not like the cold or wind. We are quite partial to this herb and we love to use it on alot of dishes.

Parmigiana di Zucchine
(Zucchini Parmesan)

Add a few Italian herbs, crushed tomatoes and the popular parmigiano and you get a mouth-watering temptation that is an absolute must to try.

6 zucchini	
6 leaves fresh basil	
1 cup crushed tomatoes	**240 ml**
2 tablespoons olive oil	**30 ml**
1¼ cups shredded mozzarella cheese	**300 ml**
½ cup grated parmigiano cheese	**120 ml**
2 teaspoons dried oregano	**10 ml**

- Preheat oven to 350° (176° C).
- Wash zucchini, cut ends off and cut lengthwise into slices. Place in oven-safe dish with 2 tablespoons (30 ml) water.
- Cover with aluminum foil and bake about 5 minutes. Remove from oven and set aside.
- Wash and chop basil. Mix basil, tomatoes, oil, salt and pepper to taste in bowl.
- Prepare baking dish with non-stick spray. Place 1 layer zucchini, 1 layer mozzarella, 1 layer parmigiano cheese, 1 layer tomato mixture and season with oregano.
- Repeat process until all ingredients are gone. Place in oven about 10 minutes or until top is golden brown. Remove from oven and cool about 10 minutes before serving.

Serves 4.

Porri al Forno
(Baked Leeks)

6 small leeks	
2 (15 ounce) cans vegetable broth	**2 (425 g)**
¼ cup flour	**60 ml**
2 tablespoons grated parmigano cheese	**30 ml**
Dash of nutmeg	
3 eggs	
1 cup milk	**240 ml**
1 tablespoon olive oil	**15 ml**

- Preheat oven to 400° (204° C).
- Clean leeks and discard root and green leaves. Wash thoroughly under running water. Cut in half lengthwise.
- Bring large pot filled with vegetable broth to boil. Place leeks in broth and cook over low heat for 10 minutes.
- Remove leeks and set aside to drain on kitchen cloth. Set broth aside.
- Combine flour, salt to taste, parmigiano cheese, nutmeg and eggs in separate bowl. Whisk and gradually add milk and equal amount of broth.
- Cover bottom of oven-safe dish with olive oil. Place leeks in dish and pour mixture over top. Place in oven and bake for 30 minutes.

Serves 4.

The **leek** belongs to the onion family, but it has its own distinct, sweet flavor. They are delicate vegetables that can be combined with other ingredients and cooked in a variety of ways including baking, braising and simmering in soups.

Asparagi al Burro
(Asparagus Sautéed in Butter)

This recipe is a perfect companion for any main course and is quickly prepared. The asparagus is sautéed in butter just as Julius Caesar requested in Lombardy.

1 pound fresh asparagus	**.5 kg**
4 tablespoons butter	**60 ml**
½ cup grated parmigiano cheese	**120 ml**

- Wash and break off ends of asparagus. Steam about 3 to 4 minutes and pierce with fork. (Asparagus should be tender, but not mushy.)
- Melt butter in skillet. Add asparagus and parmigiano cheese. Mix well and add salt and pepper to taste. Serve hot.

Serve 4.

Legend has it that Emperor Caesar Augustus would demand that tasks be done *velocius quam asparagi conquantur,* meaning "quicker than you can cook asparagus".

Insalata Russa
(Russian Salad)

This recipe is particularly satisfying during the summertime since it is served cold. A symbolic dish from the Piemonte region of Italy, Insalata Russa is full of colorful garden vegetables and a creamy mayonnaise mixture made from scratch.

2 potatoes	
10 baby carrots	
½ cup green beans	**120 ml**
½ cup frozen peas	**120 ml**
3 egg yolks	
¼ cup lemon juice, divided	**60 ml**
2 cups corn oil	**480 ml**
3 dill pickles	
1 tablespoon capers	**15 ml**

- Wash and dry potatoes and carrots and cut into cubes. Remove ends from green beans and cut into ½-inch (1.2 cm) pieces.
- Bring large pot filled with water and a little rock salt to boil. Place potatoes in boiling water and cook about 5 minutes.
- Use slotted spoon to remove potatoes from water and set aside to dry on kitchen cloth.
- Place carrots in water and cook about 8 minutes. Remove with slotted spoon and set aside to dry. Repeat process with green beans.
- Place frozen peas in same water and cook for 5 minutes. Remove with slotted spoon and set aside to dry.
- Combine egg yolks, salt and pepper to taste and half of lemon juice in separate bowl and whisk. Continue to whisk while gradually adding corn oil and remaining lemon juice.
- Finely chop pickles and capers. Place in large bowl with all vegetables and mayonnaise mixture. Mix thoroughly.
- Place mixture on serving platter and chill for 30 minutes prior to serving.

Serves 8.

Broccoletti con Aglio
(Sautéed Broccoli with Garlic)

In Italy this dish is prepared with broccoli rabe or rapini, similar to broccoli, but with thin stalks and small clusters of buds. If you happen to be lucky enough to find rapini, please use it. Otherwise, traditional broccoli is used in this very simple, yet tasty side dish with very little preparation.

1½ pounds broccoli	**680 g**
2-3 tablespoons olive oil	**30-45 ml**
1 tablespoon garlic, peeled, crushed	**15 ml**

- Wash broccoli and remove stems. Cut any wide stalks in half and steam broccoli about 8 to 12 minutes.
- Gently heat olive oil and garlic in frying pan. Add broccoli, cook about 4 minutes and turn broccoli to coat in oil. Season with salt and pepper to taste. Serve hot.

Serves 4.

Tip: If you like to spice things up a bit, try adding some crushed red pepper.

Insalata di Pomodori e Citrioli
(Tomato and Cucumber Salad)

What a great way to use tomatoes and cucumbers when they are at their peak flavor! This is a super summer salad that is light and refreshing.

6 ripe Roma tomatoes	
2 small cucumbers, sliced	
½ cup chopped red onion	**120 ml**
4 fresh basil leaves	
3 tablespoons olive oil	**45 ml**
1 tablespoon balsamic vinegar	**15 ml**

- Cut tomatoes into bite-size pieces and slice cucumbers. Place in serving bowl.
- Add onion, basil, olive oil, vinegar and salt and pepper to taste.
- Toss and mix well. Chill in refrigerator before serving.

Serves 4.

Piselli con Proscuitto Cotto
(Sautéed Peas with Ham)

Try these peas cooked Roman-style. It's an absolute must. The simple preparation and quick cooking time make the recipe even more attractive.

3 tablespoons olive oil	**45 ml**
¼ cup chopped onion	**60 ml**
½ cup diced ham	**120 ml**
1 (10 ounces) package frozen peas, thawed	**280 g**

- Heat oil and onions in skillet over medium heat until onions are translucent.
- Add ham and sauté about 3 minutes. Add peas, ¼ cup (60 ml) water, salt and pepper to taste.
- Cover and cook over medium heat about 10 to 15 minutes.

Serves 4.

Sformato di Verdure
(Baked Vegetables)

This is a perfect example of how Italians create a healthy dish infused with aromatic herbs and melted cheese without the pomp and circumstance of elaborate preparation. This is wholesome goodness at its best.

2 potatoes, peeled	
2 zucchinis, sliced	
2 tomatoes, sliced	
1 eggplant, sliced	
2 squash, sliced	
2-3 tablespoons olive oil, divided	**30-45 ml**
4 cups shredded mozzarella cheese, divided	**1 L**
4 leaves fresh basil, chopped	

- Preheat oven to 350° (176° C).
- Slice all vegetables about ¼-inch (.6 cm) thick and set aside.
- Drizzle olive oil on the bottom of 9 x 13-inch (23 x 33 cm) dish and layer vegetables one at a time. Sprinkle with salt and pepper to taste and mozzarella cheese. Drizzle more olive oil over top.
- Continue layers until dish is almost to full. Top with remaining mozzarella cheese.
- Bake about 35 to 45 minutes. Remove from oven and cool a few minutes before serving. Garnish with basil. Enjoy!

Serves 4 to 6.

Verdure all Griglia
(Grilled Vegetables with Basil)

Olive oil and a basil mixture coats an assortment of fresh vegetables and grilling seals in the flavor. The temptation to try this recipe should not be resisted. It can easily be served with any chicken or beef recipe.

3 tablespoons olive oil	**45 ml**
8 leaves fresh basil, chopped	
1 garlic clove, peeled, minced	
2 small eggplant	
3 zucchinis	
2 red, green or yellow bell peppers	
3 Roma tomatoes	

- Preheat oven to 400° (204° C).
- Combine olive oil, basil, garlic, salt and pepper to taste in small bowl. Stir to mix well and set aside.
- Cut eggplant and zucchini into thin slices, peppers into strips and tomatoes into quarters. Arrange peppers and eggplant on baking sheet.
- Grill in oven about 5 minutes on each side. Remove from oven, place zucchinis and tomatoes in oven and cook about 2 minutes on each side. Remove from oven.
- Arrange all vegetables on serving platter. Pour olive oil mixture over top. Serve warm.

Serves 4.

Melanzane al Funghetto
(Sautéed Eggplant)

Melanzane al Funghetto is "eggplant cooked in the style of mushrooms".
After cooking, the cubed pieces of eggplant look like mushrooms. Olive oil,
garlic and tomatoes add to its wonderful flavor.

2 medium eggplants	
3 tablespoons olive oil	**45 ml**
2 cloves garlic, peeled, crushed	
1 (14 ounce) can crushed tomatoes	**396 g**
1 tablespoon chopped fresh parsley	**15 ml**

- Cut eggplant into cubes and set aside.
- Combine olive oil, garlic, tomatoes, salt and pepper to taste in skillet. Sauté about 10 minutes.
- Add eggplant and stir to mix well. Reduce heat, simmer for 20 to 25 minutes or until eggplant is tender and stir occasionally. If eggplant sticks, add ¼ cup (60 ml) water and stir.
- Place eggplant mixture in serving bowl. Sprinkle parsley and serve hot.

Serves 4 to 6.

Carciofini al Forno
(Baked Baby Artichokes)

This side dish is wonderful when paired with any meat, pork or poultry recipe. The artichokes are tender and savory baked in the oven and topped with breadcrumbs.

14 baby artichokes	
2 cloves garlic, peeled, crushed	
¼ cup olive oil	**60 ml**
¾ cup white wine	**180 ml**

Topping:

1½ cups breadcrumbs	**360 ml**
1 tablespoon fresh lemon juice	**15 ml**
2 tablespoons finely chopped fresh parsley	**30 ml**
Olive oil	

- Preheat oven to 375° (190° C).
- Peel artichoke stems, chop off top one-third and peel off outer, tough leaves. Keep prepared artichokes in bowl of water with a little lemon added to prevent discoloration.
- In casserole dish large enough for all artichokes, add artichokes, garlic, 2 tablespoons (30 ml) olive oil and white wine. Add a little water if needed to bring level up to almost cover artichokes, cover and bake until tender, about 20 to 30 minutes.
- Remove artichokes from oven and increase temperature to 425° (220° C). Pour off any excess liquid from cooked artichokes.
- Mix all ingredients for topping and sprinkle over artichokes in casserole dish. Drizzle on additional olive oil and bake artichokes just until topping is golden brown.

Serves 4.

Stuzzichini
Fun Side Dishes

— *Semplicemente per*
il piacere di mangiare! —

— *Simply for your*
eating pleasure. —

Supplí
(Fried Risotto Balls)

It is impossible to wander through the streets of Rome without seeing one of the many local pizzerie where this specialty is sold. You cannot say you have been to Italy if you have not tried them. You will agree that the homemade version is no less memorable.

1 recipe Risotto con Sugo di Carne (page 58)
2 eggs
4 tablespoons grated parmigiano cheese   **60 ml**
¾ cup shredded mozzarella cheese   **180 ml**
Breadcrumbs
Cooking oil

- Prepare Risotto con Sugo di Carne on page 58 and cool before adding more ingredients.
- Add eggs and parmigiano cheese and mix thoroughly using hands.
- Take handful of rice in one hand and a pinch of mozzarella with other hand and push it into center of rice mixture. Mold rice mixture into egg shape.
- Continue to repeat process until all mixture is gone. Roll each supplí into breadcrumbs, coat all sides well and set aside.
- Heat cooking oil over medium heat. (Oil should be very hot before cooking.) Fry supplí, turning frequently, to cook well on all sides. Remove from oil and drain on paper towels. Serve hot.

Serves 6.

Crocchette di Patate
(Breaded Potatoes with Ham and Cheese)

The secret to making crocchette successfully is using the right type of potato. Enjoy this mouth-watering specialty any time as the center of your meal or just as a snack.

2 pounds Yukon potatoes	**1 kg**
2 eggs	
2-3 tablespoons grated parmigiano cheese	**30-45 ml**
Dash of nutmeg	
2-3 slices ham, diced	
3-4 cups shredded mozzarella cheese	**710-960 ml**
Breadcrumbs	
Cooking oil	

- Wash, peel and cut potatoes in half. Boil potatoes until tender, about 30 to 45 minutes. Drain and set aside until completely cool.
- Once potatoes cool, mash thoroughly until texture is as smooth as possible.
- Add eggs, parmigiano, salt and pepper to taste and nutmeg. Mix well with hands.
- Take handful of potato mixture in one hand and pinch of mozzarella and ham with other hand and push it into center of potato mixture. Mold into egg shape. Repeat process until all mixture is gone.
- Roll each crocchette into breadcrumbs and coat all sides well. Set aside.
- Heat cooking oil over medium heat. (Oil should be very hot before cooking.)
- Fry crocchette, turning frequently to cook well on all sides. Remove from oil and drain on paper towels. Serve hot.

Serves 4 to 6.

Impasto per la Pizza

(Basic Pizza Dough For Bread Machine, Food Processor and By Hand)

Ingredients for Bread Machine:

3½ cups flour, divided	830 ml
1 cup warm water	240 ml
2 tablespoons yeast	30 ml
¼ teaspoon sugar	1 ml
¼ cup olive oil	60 ml
1 teaspoon salt	5 ml

Directions for Bread Machine:

- (Please refer to user's manual for best settings.) Add ingredients to bread machine bin in order listed above (unless user's manual specifies otherwise).
- Turn to dough setting, push start and complete full cycle. When complete, place dough in floured bowl and cool to room temperature before rolling out.

Serves 4.

Directions for Food Processor:

- (Use dough blade or cutting blade.) Pour 1 cup (240 ml) warm water (at least 85° to 115°/50°C) in processor. Add sugar and salt and mix on low about 15 to 20 seconds.
- Add yeast and mix on low again for about 5 to 10 seconds. Add 1 cup (240 ml) flour and mix on low for 10 to 15 seconds.
- Add olive oil and mix until they blend well. Add remaining flour and mix on high until the dough turns into ball.
- Turn machine off, open it and touch dough to check its texture. If dough is too wet, add 1 tablespoon (15 ml) flour and mix again on high. Continue adding 1 tablespoon (15 ml) flour at a time until dough is right consistency.
- If dough is too dry, add 1 tablespoon (15 ml) water and mix again on high. Continue adding 1 tablespoon (15 ml) water at a time until dough is the right consistency.
- Remove dough from food processor and place on floured surface. Knead dough for about 1 to 2 minutes, form into ball and

(Continued on next page.)

(*Continued*)

place in bowl covered with lightly moist paper towel. Store bowl in warm, dry area to rise for about 45 minutes.

• When dough doubles, punch it down to release air and knead for additional 1 to 2 minutes. Place covered bowl with dough in warm, dry area for additional 1 to 1½ hours to rise again. Dough is ready to roll out.

Directions for Hand Preparation:

• Pour warm water (must be at least 85° to 115°/50°C) into bowl. Add sugar and salt and mix until they blend well. Add yeast and mix again. Set aside for about 5 minutes.

• Add 1 cup (240 ml) flour and olive oil and blend well. Add remaining flour and mix well until dough turns into ball.

• If dough is too wet, add 1 tablespoon (15 ml) flour and mix again on high. Continue adding 1 tablespoon (15 ml) flour at a time until dough is right consistency.

• If dough is too dry, add 1 tablespoon (15 ml) water and mix again on high. Continue adding 1 tablespoon (15 ml) water at a time until dough is right consistency.

• Place dough on floured surface and knead dough about 1 to 2 minutes. Form into ball, place into bowl and cover with lightly moist paper towel. Store bowl in warm, dry area about 45 minutes to rise.

• When dough doubles in size, punch down to release air and knead for additional 1 to 2 minutes. Place covered bowl with dough in warm, dry area for additional 1 to 1½ hours to rise again. Dough is now ready to roll.

Directions for Rolling Dough:

• (Method to roll dough is same for bread machine, food processor or hand preparation.) Place dough on floured surface.

• If mixture appears too sticky, sprinkle extra flour over top. Place both hands in center and press outward and turn clockwise. Continue process until dough is about ½-inch (1.2 cm) thick.

• Use rolling pin to roll to about ¼-inch (.6 cm) thick. Carefully transfer dough to greased baking sheet prepared with non-stick spray.

• Use fork to puncture some holes in dough to prevent bubbling. Dough is ready for toppings.

Pizza con Patate e Rosmarino
(Pizza with Potato and Rosemary)

A delicious pizza without tomatoes…. imagine that! We know it may be hard to picture pizza without cheese or tomatoes, but this recipe is an absolute delicacy.

1 recipe Impasto per la Pizza, rolled out (page 132)
Olive oil
1 large potato, thinly sliced
1-2 springs fresh rosemary

- Preheat to 400° (204° C).
- Brush some of olive oil on pizza dough. Sprinkle salt and pepper to taste and arrange potatoes and rosemary. Place in oven.
- Bake about 30 minutes, remove from oven and cool slightly. Cut into wedges. Enjoy!

Serves 4.

Pizza ai Tre Formaggi
(Three-Cheese Pizza)

Pizza can really be topped with just about anything, but the flavors of these three cheeses blend so well it would be sinful not to experience this fabulous recipe.

1 recipe Impasto per la Pizza, rolled out (page 132)	
3 tablespoons olive oil, divided	**45 ml**
½ cup shredded mozzarella cheese	**120 ml**
½ cup shredded fontina cheese	**120 ml**
½ cup crumbled gorgonzola cheese	**120 ml**
2 leaves fresh basil, chopped	

- Preheat oven to 400° (204° C).
- Brush some of olive oil on pizza dough, sprinkle a little salt on top and arrange three cheeses on it.
- Drizzle remaining olive oil over pizza and place in oven. Bake about 30 minutes.
- Remove pizza from oven, sprinkle chopped basil over top and cut into wedges. Enjoy!

Serves 4.

Pizza con Salsicce
(Pizza with Sausage)

Pizza is the best-known Italian dish in the world. Almost everyone has tasted pizza at least once in his life, but we can promise you have never tasted anything like this pizza. It's truly unique and truly Italian!

1 recipe Impasto per la Pizza, rolled out (page 132)	
1 (28 ounce) can whole peeled or crushed tomatoes with juice	**794 g**
1½ cups shredded mozzarella cheese	**360 ml**
1½ cups Italian sausage without casings	**360 ml**
1 teaspoon dried oregano	**5 ml**
3 tablespoons olive oil, divided	**45 ml**

- Preheat oven to 400° (204° C).
- Spread tomatoes evenly over pizza dough. Sprinkle mozzarella cheese over top, then sausage.
- Add oregano and drizzle olive oil evenly over entire pizza. Add salt and pepper to taste. Bake about 30 minutes.
- Remove from oven and let stand about 5 minutes before cutting.

Serves 4.

Pizza con Gamberetti
(Pizza with Shrimp)

This is a surprisingly easy pizza to make. It's great for any kind of gathering and it is truly amazing. It is so delicious that we know people who love this dish, but don't like seafood. It's tasty and sensational!

1 recipe Impasto per la Pizza, rolled out (page 132)	
3 tablespoons olive oil, divided	**45 ml**
1 (28 ounce) can whole peeled or crushed tomatoes with juice	**794 g**
2½ cups frozen shrimp, thawed, veined, tails removed	**600 ml**
2 cups shredded lettuce	**480 ml**
3 tablespoons mayonnaise	**45 ml**
2 leaves fresh basil, chopped	

- Preheat oven to 400° (204° C).
- Brush 1 tablespoon (15 ml) olive oil over pizza dough. Spread tomatoes and shrimp evenly over top. Drizzle remaining olive oil and sprinkle salt and pepper to taste. Bake about 30 minutes.
- While pizza bakes, place shredded lettuce and mayonnaise in bowl and mix well.
- Remove pizza from oven and set aside to cool for about 20 minutes.
- Once pizza cools enough to remove from baking dish, place on large platter. Spread lettuce and mayonnaise mixture evenly over entire pizza. Top with chopped basil and serve.

Serves 4.

Pizza Bianca con Erbe
(White Pizza with Herbs)

This is a great pizza for any meal. Its simpicity adorns any great dish you serve with it. And, it's outstanding when served alone. The aromatic flavors of the bread will change your concept of pizza forever.

1 recipe Impasto per la Pizza, rolled out (page 132)	
5 tablespoons olive oil, divided	**75 ml**
4 tablespoons mixed herbs (rosemary, basil, parsley, sage or thyme)	**60 ml**

- Preheat oven to 400° (204°).
- Brush 2 tablespoons (30 ml) olive oil on pizza dough and sprinkle some salt evenly over dough. Distribute herb mixture evenly over dough.
- Drizzle remaining olive oil and some pepper to taste and place in oven. Bake about 30 minutes. Crust should be a nice golden brown.

Serves 4.

Tip: Use fresh herbs, if possible, because they are so flavorful.

Timo (Thyme) is an herb consisting of clusters of tiny green leaves on a thin, woody stem. Its flavor can overpower some foods, so it is best to add a little at a time. It can either be added to a recipe whole or the leaves can be chopped. Thyme is a wonderful addition to stocks, sauces and soups.

Pizza Margherita

There is a famous legend that goes along with this pizza and all Italians love it. As the story goes, the French could not prepare a pizza fit for a queen and the famous Italian "Pizzaiolo Raffaele Esposito" was invited to the Queen's court to prepare a proper pizza. He created a pizza with the colors of the Italian flag and this pizza was fit for royalty.

1 recipe Impasto per la Pizza, rolled out (page 132)	
3 tablespoons olive oil, divided	**45 ml**
1 (28 ounce) can whole peeled or crushed tomatoes with juice	**794 g**
1½ cups shredded mozzarella cheese	**360 ml**
8 leaves fresh basil, chopped	

- Preheat oven to 400° (204° C) .
- Brush 1 tablespoon (15 ml) olive oil on pizza dough and spread tomatoes evenly over top.
- Spread mozzarella cheese evenly over top to cover. Add salt and pepper to taste and drizzle remaining olive oil.
- Bake about 30 minutes. Remove from oven, sprinkle chopped basil over pizza and serve. Enjoy!

Serves 4.

Schiacciate con Prosciutto e Mozzarella
(Prosciutto and Mozzarella Panini)

Just one bite of this Italian-style sandwich and you will be forever addicted to it. Once the prosciutto and mozzarella are placed inside a slice of freshly baked pizza crust, eat it immediately while it's still warm and wonderful!

1 recipe Pizza Bianca con Erbe, rolled out (page 137)
Olive oil
8 slices prosciutto
8 slices fresh mozzarella

- Preheat oven to 400° (204° C).
- Brush small amount of olive oil over top of dough. Place in oven and bake about 30 minutes or until pizza crust is a nice golden brown.
- Remove from oven and cool crust before cutting. Divide pizza into quarters, slice open and place prosciutto and mozzarella inside. Serve while still warm.

Serves 4.

Schiacciate con Mozzarella e Pomodoro
(Mozzarella and Tomato Panini)

Only the freshest ingredients will do this sandwich any justice. The combined flavors of fresh mozzarella, fresh basil and fresh tomatoes is, well, refreshing to say the least.

1 recipe Pizza Bianca con Erbe, rolled out (page 137)
Olive oil
8 slices fresh mozzarella
2 tomatoes, washed, sliced
8 leaves fresh basil

- Preheat oven to 400° (204° C).
- Brush small amount of olive oil over top of dough. Place in oven and bake about 30 minutes or until pizza crust is a nice golden brown.
- Remove from oven and cool before cutting. Divide pizza crust into quarters, slice open and place mozzarella, tomato slices and basil inside.
- Sprinkle salt to taste and drizzle a little olive oil inside each panini.

Serves 4.

Schiacciate con Prosciutto Cotto e Formaggio
(Ham and Cheese Panini)

This variation is equally satisfying as the other Paninis and should definitely be put on your "must try" list. It tastes best when prepared with these delicious ingredients, but feel free to experiment with your own favorite deli selections.

1 recipe Pizza Bianca con Erbe, rolled out (page 137)
Olive oil
8 slices oven-roasted ham
8 slices provolone

* Preheat oven to 400° (204° C).
* Brush small amount of olive oil over top of dough. Place in oven and bake about 30 minutes or until crust is a nice golden brown.
* Remove from oven and cool pizza crust before cutting. Divide crust into quarters, slice open and place ham and provolone inside.
* Place back in oven for about 5 minutes or until cheese melts.

Serves 4.

Calzone con Verdure
(Vegetable Calzone)

Calzone or "trouser leg" is a tasty alternative to pizza. Typical pizza ingredients are placed on rolled-out pizza dough then the dough is folded over to a half-moon shape. This recipe is full of healthy vegetables and will definitely satisfy a hungry appetite.

3 tablespoons olive oil	**45 ml**
1 clove garlic, peeled, crushed	
1 (5 ounce) bag fresh spinach	**143 g**
1 medium eggplant, diced	
1½ cups sliced mushroom	**360 ml**
1 teaspoon crushed red pepper	**5 ml**
4 cups shredded mozzarella cheese	**.9 L**
3 tablespoons grated parmigiano cheese	**45 ml**
1 recipe Impasto per la Pizza, (page 132)	
Olive oil	

- Preheat oven to 400° (204° C).
- Heat olive oil and garlic in non-stick skillet over medium heat. Add spinach, eggplant, mushrooms, salt to taste and crushed red pepper. Drain skillet and add mozzarella cheese and parmigiano cheese. Stir to mix well.
- Place ball of dough on floured surface and divide into 4 balls. Roll each ball into flat circle about ½-inch (1.2 cm) thick. Brush olive oil over each circle and sprinkle a little salt over top.
- Divide vegetable filling on each of 4 circles. Place filling on half of each circle and leave 1-inch (2.5 cm) border.
- Fold other half of circle over filling and pinch edges to seal.
- Spray non-stick spray on baking sheet and place each calzone on baking sheet. Brush olive oil on outside of each calzone.
- Place in oven and bake about 30 minutes. Check occasionally to make sure calzones are browning nicely.

Serves 4.

Calzone di Ricotta e Prosciutto
(Ham and Ricotta Calzone)

Calzone di Ricotta e Prosciutto is a classic calzone recipe. You can use this recipe as a starting point then experiment with favorite ingredients to create your own winning combination.

2 cups ricotta cheese, drained	**480 ml**
4 slices prosciutto cotto, cut into strips	
2 cups shredded mozzarella cheese	**480 ml**
3 tablespoons grated parmigiano cheese	**45 ml**
1 recipe Impasto per la Pizza (page 132)	
Olive oil	

- Preheat oven to 400° (204° C).
- Combine drained ricotta, diced ham, mozzarella, parmigiano and salt and pepper to taste in large bowl. Stir to mix well and set aside.
- Place ball of dough on floured surface and divide into 4 balls. Roll each ball into flat circle about ½-inch (1.2 cm) thick. Brush olive oil over each circle and sprinkle a little salt over top.
- Divide filling among 4 circles, place filling on half of each circle and leave 1-inch (2.5 cm) border. Fold other half of circle over filling and pinch edges to seal.
- Spray non-stick spray on baking sheet and place each calzone on baking sheet. Brush olive oil on outside of each calzone. Place in oven and bake about 30 minutes.

Serves 4.

Frittata con Patate
(Frittata with Potatoes)

Frittata is an Italian-style omelette. A variety of fillings mix with eggs instead of being folded inside. The frittata is then cut into wedges and eaten either hot or cold.

8 eggs
3 tablespoons olive oil   **45 ml**
1 medium potato, thinly sliced
Grated parmigiano cheese

- Beat eggs with wire whisk for 2 to 3 minutes in medium bowl. Add salt and pepper to taste, mix well and set aside.
- Heat olive oil in large non-stick skillet over medium heat. Add thin potato slices and sauté until tender.
- Pour egg mixture into skillet, cover and cook over medium heat. When edges are firm, separate egg from skillet with spatula. Tilt skillet so uncooked egg on top runs to bottom of skillet and cooks.
- When egg mixture is no longer runny on top, place large plate over skillet and flip frittata so that cooked part is facing up. Slide uncooked side into skillet to finish cooking.
- Remove frittata from skillet onto plate and sprinkle parmigiano cheese over top Cut into wedges and serve.

Serves 4 to 6.

Frittata con Asparagi
(Frittata with Asparagus)

Sautéing asparagus heightens the flavors and soft texture of this frittata. That's one reason why this frittata is so popular.

8 eggs	
2 tablespoons grated parmigiano cheese	**30 ml**
3 tablespoons olive oil	**45 ml**
6 stalks asparagus, cut into small pieces	

- Beat eggs with wire whisk for 2 to 3 minutes in medium bowl. Add parmigiano, salt and pepper to taste and mix well. Set aside.
- Heat olive oil in large non-stick skillet over medium heat. Add asparagus and sauté until tender.
- Pour egg mixture into skillet, cover and cook over medium heat.
- When edges are firm, separate egg from skillet with spatula. Tilt skillet so uncooked egg on top runs to bottom of skillet and cooks.
- When egg mixture is no longer runny on top, place large plate over skillet and flip frittata so that cooked part is facing up. Slide uncooked side into skillet to finish cooking.
- Remove frittata from skillet onto plate, cut into wedges and serve.

Serves 4 to 6.

Ancient Romans held **asparagus** in high regard because of its unique flavor and texture. They ate it fresh when it was in season and were the first to preserve it by freezing it in the snowline of the Alps.

Frittata con Zucchine e Cipolle
(Frittata with Zucchini and Onions)

If you are not sure what to do with that zucchini and onion sitting in the refrigerator, we have a solution. Just mix these 2 vegetables into your egg mixture for a delicious Italian-style omelet.

8 eggs
3 tablespoons olive oil   **45 ml**
1 large zucchini, thinly sliced
1 small onion, thinly sliced

- Beat eggs with wire whisk for 2 to 3 minutes in medium bowl. Add salt and pepper to taste and mix well.

- Heat olive oil in large non-stick skillet over medium heat. Add zucchini slices and onion and sauté until tender.

- Pour egg mixture into skillet, cover and cook over medium heat. When edges are firm, separate egg from skillet with spatula. Tilt skillet so uncooked egg on top runs to bottom of skillet and cooks.

- When egg mixture is no longer runny on top, place large plate over skillet and flip frittata so that cooked part is facing up. Slide uncooked side into skillet to finish cooking.

- Remove frittata from skillet onto plate, cut into wedges and serve.

Serves 4 to 6.

Frittata con Formaggi
(Frittata with Cheese)

In case you didn't have time to run to the store for fresh vegetables today, you can still have your frittata with a few Italian cheeses thrown in. This recipe will easily melt in your mouth.

8 eggs	
1 cup shredded mozzarella cheese	**240 ml**
3 tablespoons grated parmigiano cheese	**45 ml**
1 cup diced fontina cheese	**240 ml**

- Beat eggs with wire whisk for 2 to 3 minutes in medium bowl. Add salt and pepper to taste and mix well.

- Spray large non-stick skillet with non-stick spray, pour egg mixture into skillet, cover and cook over medium heat.

- When edges are firm, separate egg from skillet with spatula. Tilt skillet so uncooked egg on top runs to bottom of skillet and cooks.

- When egg mixture is no longer runny on top, place large plate over skillet and flip frittata so that cooked part is facing up. Slide uncooked side into skillet to finish cooking.

- Add mozzarella, parmigiano and fontina cheese, cover and continue to cook for 1 to 2 minutes until cheeses melt. Remove frittata from skillet onto plate. Cut into wedges and serve.

Serves 4 to 6.

Fritto Misto di Verdure
(Fried Vegetables)

A variety of fresh vegetables is bathed in a creamy batter and fried to golden brown perfection. When Mamma makes these, you must have very fast reflexes because it doesn't take long for these appetizing veggies to disappear right off the platter.

Cooking oil	
1½ cups broccoli florets	**360 ml**
1½ cups cauliflower florets	**360 ml**
2 medium zucchini, sliced	
1 egg, beaten	
1 cup flour	**240 ml**
Beer or sparkling mineral water	

- Heat cooking oil in large, deep skillet over medium heat and cover.
- Wash vegetables, cut into bite-size pieces and dry with paper towel. Set aside.
- Mix egg, flour and beer or sparkling mineral water in medium bowl. Stir continually and add salt and pepper to taste.
- (Batter should stick to fork without completely running off. If batter is too runny, add a little flour. If batter is too thick, add a little more beer or water.)
- Dip vegetables into batter and completely coat. Carefully place vegetables into hot oil and cook on all sides until light brown.
- Remove with slotted spoon and drain on paper towels. Sprinkle vegetables with salt to taste and serve.

Serves 4 to 6.

Dolci
Desserts

— E per finire…procedere con
cautela, state per entrare in
"zona deliziosa"! —

— And for the end…proceed with
caution, you are about to enter
the "delicious zone"! —

Frappe
(Fried Sweet Dough)

Frappe is lightly sweetened dough fried until it puffs up then dusted with powdered sugar. It was originally created for Carnevale (carnival), the period of time between Epiphany and Ash Wednesday. During this period of merriment, people celebrated with parties, parades, floats, masks and of course, food. Different regions have different names for this fritter-like pastry: Cenci in Tuscany, Bugie in Genoa, and Frappe in Emilia.

3 cups flour	**710 ml**
3 eggs	
1 cup sugar	**240 ml**
Dash of nutmeg	
¼ teaspoon grated lemon rind	**1 ml**
½ cup Grand Marnier	**120 ml**
1 cup cooking oil	**240 ml**
Powdered sugar	

- Mix flour and eggs in large bowl. Beat by hand until they blend well.
- Add sugar, dash of salt, nutmeg, lemon rind and Grand Marnier. Batter should be thick consistency.
- Heat oil in large, deep frying pan over medium heat and cover. Scoop about 2 tablespoons (30 ml) batter into large spoon. Drizzle batter into oil to form a line. Batter will cook very quickly so watch closely.
- Turn frequently to cook on both sides. Frappe is done when both sides are golden brown.
- Remove frappe with slotted spoon and drain on paper towels while others cook.
- Sprinkle powdered sugar over frappe and serve warm.

Serves 4 to 6.

Tip: Frappe can be made 1-2 days ahead and stored at room temperature in an airtight container.

Castagnole
(Italian Cake Doughnut Holes)

Castagnole are fried dough balls lightly sweetened with liqueur and lemon zest. When Mamma makes a batch of these, they disappear before they even make it to the dinner table. They are also very popular during Carnevale (carnival).

2 cups flour	**480 ml**
2 eggs	
½ cup sugar	**120 ml**
1 tablespoon powdered sugar	**15 ml**
1 tablespoon cake yeast	**15 ml**
3 tablespoons butter, melted	**45 ml**
2 teaspoons vanilla extract	**10 ml**
½ teaspoon orange rind, grated	**2 ml**
4 tablespoons marsala wine	**60 ml**
Cooking oil	
Powdered sugar	

- Mix flour, eggs, sugar, powdered sugar, yeast, dash of salt, butter, vanilla and orange rind in a large bowl with wooden spoon. Stir to mix well.
- Pour in marsala wine slowly until dough forms. Dough should not be too hard or too soft. Work dough for approximately 10 minutes.
- Cut into chunks and roll into cylinders about width of 1 finger. Cut into 1-inch pieces and mold into balls.
- Heat cooking oil in large, deep skillet over medium heat. (The castagnole need to float in oil so be sure to have plenty of oil.)
- Place castagnole in oil to fry. When castagnole puff out, remove from oil and drain on paper towels. Sprinkle powdered sugar and serve.

Serves 4 to 6.

Ciambellone
(Italian Bundt Cake)

Ciambellone is a ring cake and one of the most common types of Italian cake. It is a dry cake and is great for dipping in wine. If, and it is a big if, there is any leftover, Ciambellone makes a great breakfast companion with a cup of hot coffee or espresso.

4 eggs	
1 cup sugar	**240 ml**
¼ cup orange juice	**60 ml**
1 cup vanilla yogurt	**240 ml**
⅔ cup sunflower oil	**160 ml**
1½ cups flour	**360 ml**
1 tablespoon cake yeast	**15 ml**
Powdered sugar	

- Whisk eggs thoroughly in large bowl. Add sugar, orange juice and dash of salt. Continue to mix well until texture is smooth and silky.
- Gradually incorporate remaining ingredients.
- Preheat oven to 375° (190° C).
- Prepare bundt pan with non-stick spray and pour in cake mixture. Place in oven and bake about 50 minutes.
- Insert toothpick into center of cake. If it comes out clean, the cake is done. Remove from oven and cool before removing from pan.
- To enhance presentation, sprinkle with powdered sugar and serve.

Serves 4 to 6.

Fragole Dolci
(Strawberries with Sugar and Lemon)

This is a delightfully sweet and light way to end a hearty Italian meal. The strawberry dessert can be prepared ahead of time and kept chilled until ready to serve. Another variation enjoyed by Italians is to use balsamic vinegar instead of freshly squeezed lemon and orange juice.

1 pound strawberries, sliced	**.5 kg**
⅓ cup sugar	**80 ml**
½ lemon, freshly squeezed	
½ orange, freshly squeezed	

- Wash strawberries thoroughly and slice strawberries in medium bowl.
- Sprinkle sugar, lemon juice and orange juice over strawberries and mix well. Serve chilled.

Serves 4 to 6.

Crostata
(Italian Jam Tart)

Crostata is a jam tart consisting of a shortbread crust covered with any flavor jam followed by a woven pattern of more shortbread crust. It is a very satisfying dessert our whole family looks forward to. There are never any leftovers.

1¾ cups flour	420 ml
2 egg yolks, beaten	
½ cup salted butter, melted	120 ml
½ cup sugar	120 ml
1 tablespoon grated lemon zest	15 ml
1¼ cups fruit jam	300 ml

- Combine flour, eggs and butter in large bowl. Mix until they blend well. Add sugar and lemon zest.
- Continue mixing until dough forms. Separate dough into 2 parts with one slightly larger than the other. Cover with plastic wrap and place in refrigerator for 1 hour.
- Preheat oven to 350° (176° C).
- Use larger part to cover the bottom and sides of shallow, buttered 9-inch (23 cm) tart pan. Spread jam evenly over entire surface.
- Roll out remaining dough on lightly floured surface and cut 6 to 8 strips about ½-inch (1.2 cm) thick.
- Lay 3 to 4 strips lengthwise and weave remaining strips across top. Place on middle rack and cook for 30 minutes or until crust is light, golden brown.

Serves 4 to 6.

Torta di Pere alla Cannella
(Cinnamon-Pear Tart)

Just as in ancient times, cinnamon is treasured as the key ingredient in this scrumptious fruit tart.

½ **cup flour**	**120 ml**
¼ **cup unsweetened apple juice**	**60 ml**
2 **tablespoons corn oil**	**30 ml**
4 **Barlett pears**	
4 **sticks cinnamon**	
3 **tablespoons brown sugar, divided**	**45 ml**

- Preheat oven to 350° (176° C).
- Combine flour, a little salt, apple juice and oil in mixing bowl. Stir to mix well until smooth, elastic texture appears. Pour mixture onto parchment paper. Place in refrigerator for 30 minutes.
- Remove from refrigerator and roll out on lightly floured surface. Place in buttered 9-inch (23 cm) tart pan. Work dough so it covers bottom and sides evenly.
- Place in oven about 15 minutes. Remove and set aside.
- Peel and slice pears. Place 2 sliced pears in small pan dish and sprinkle with cinnamon and half of sugar.
- Cook and stir over medium heat for 10 minutes or until pureed. Remove cinnamon sticks and discard.
- Fill crust with pear puree. Arrange remaining sliced pears on top of puree. Sprinkle with remaining sugar.
- Place back in oven about 20 minutes. Serve warm or cold.

Serves 4 to 6.

> In ancient times, cannella or **cinnamon**, was used for medicinal purposes and flavoring for beverages. It was considered to be more precious than gold. In medieval Europe, cinnamon was a staple ingredient and the demand for it drove many explorers to travel to distant lands in search of it.

Torta Panna e Miele
(Honey-Whip Cream Cake)

This cake recipe can be combined with many different ingredients to create a wide variety of desserts. The recipe uses honey to produce a unique flavor sure to be a hit with your family and friends.

5 tablespoons olive oil	75 ml
3 tablespoons packed brown sugar	45 ml
1 ounce honey	28 ml
⅓ cup chopped walnuts	80 ml
2 ounces all-purpose flour	57 g
1½ ounces corn flour	45 g
1 egg yolk	
Whipped cream	

- Preheat oven to 325° (162° C).
- Whisk oil, brown sugar and honey in small bowl. Mix until they blend well.
- Place walnuts on baking sheet and toast in oven for 5 to 8 minutes.
- Add ¼ cup (60 ml) toasted nuts to sugar-honey mixture. Stir to mix well. Add flour, egg yolk and a little salt and mix thoroughly.
- Cover oven-safe dish with parchment paper. Pour cake mixture into dish and place in oven to bake for 20 minutes.
- Remove from oven and place on cooling rack to cool. Decorate with whipping cream and sprinkle with remaining nuts. Serve and enjoy.

Serves 4.

Spiedini di Frutta al Cioccolato
(Fruit Kabobs with Chocolate)

Italians love fresh foods, especially fresh fruits. In the small towns on market days, the fruit carts are overflowing with colorful fresh fruit. This simple fresh fruit dessert is enhanced by the mouth-watering chocolate mixture.

Juice of 1 lemon	
3 bananas	
2 cups strawberries	**480 ml**
1 cup blueberries	**240 ml**
1 cup cherries	**240 ml**
1½ cups dark chocolate	**360 ml**
2 tablespoons rum	**30 ml**
1 teaspoon cinnamon	**5 ml**

- Cut lemon in half and squeeze juice from it. Peel bananas, cut into bite-size pieces and drizzle lemon juice over them.
- Clean and dry rest of fruit. Place on skewer alternating fruit.

- Melt chocolate in little pot over low heat. Pour in rum and cinnamon.
- Arrange fruit kabobs on platter and serve with warm chocolate for dipping.

Serves 4.

Torta di Mele
(Apple Cake)

Another family favorite, Torta di Mele, is usually gobbled up immediately after dinner with only a few crumbs left behind. It is similar to the Ciambellone, but is made in a regular cake pan instead of a bundt-style pan.

1 ½ **cups flour**	**360 ml**
1 **cup sugar**	**240 ml**
3 **eggs**	
½ **cup (1 stick) butter, softened**	**120 ml**
¼ **teaspoon grated lemon rind**	**1 ml**
1 **tablespoon cake yeast**	**15 ml**
5 **Granny Smith apples, peeled, sliced**	
Powdered sugar	

- Combine flour, sugar and eggs in large bowl and mix thoroughly. Add butter and stir to mix well.
- Add lemon rind and cake yeast. Mix until all ingredients blend well.
- Preheat oven to 375° (190° C).
- Prepare round cake pan with non-stick spray. Pour in cake batter and spread evenly in pan. Place apple slices over batter and push some slices into batter.
- Place in oven and bake about 40 to 50 minutes. Insert toothpick into center of cake. If it comes out clean, the cake is done.
- Remove from oven and cool before removing from pan. To enhance presentation, sprinkle with powdered sugar and serve.

Serves 4 to 6.

Macedonia
(Italian Fruit Salad)

In Italy, fruit alone is considered a dessert. It is common to find a bowl of fruit present at every meal in a home or restaurant. This recipe is a typical fruit salad that combines the fresh fruits of the season to produce a sweet, but healthy after-dinner treat.

2 small apples	
1 banana	
1 small pear	
½ cup black seedless grapes	**120 ml**
½ cup green grapes	**120 ml**
1 peach	
1 nectarine	
2 apricots	
½ cup strawberries	**120 ml**
½ cup raspberries	**120 ml**
Juice of 2 lemons	
Juice of 4 oranges	
Sugar, optional	
3 tablespoons Grand Marnier, optional	**45 ml**

- Wash, peel and slice fruit into bite-size pieces. Leave washed grapes and raspberries whole.
- Combine all fruit, lemon juice and orange juice in large bowl and stir well.
- Add sugar and Grand Marnier, if desired, and stir thoroughly.
- Cover bowl and refrigerate about 30 minutes to 1 hour. Serve chilled.

Serves 6.

Torta Morbida all Ananas
(Pineapple Cake)

This is a great dessert that satisfies your sweet tooth with fresh fruit. The recipe resembles the American version of a pineapple-upside-down cake.

½ **cup butter, softened**	**120 ml**
½ **cup sugar**	**120 ml**
1 egg	
2 egg yolks	
⅓ **cup flour**	**80 ml**
2 tablespoons chopped almonds	**30 ml**
1 whole lemon rind, grated	
8-10 slices pineapple	

- Mix butter with sugar, add egg and egg yolks one at a time and mix well after each addition. Do not add additional egg until mixture is smooth.
- Gradually add flour, almonds and lemon rind. Mix until they blend well and texture is smooth.
- Preheat oven to 350° (176° C).
- Grease and flour oven-safe dish. Pour mixture into dish. (Be sure it is nice and level.)
- Place pineapples over top. Bake in oven about 45 minutes. Insert toothpick into cake. If toothpick comes out clean, cake is done. Cool before serving.

Serves 4.

Ciambellone con Nutella
(Nutella Chocolate Cake)

The word ciambellone comes from the word ciambella meaning doughnut. This particular version is not fried like a doughnut, but baked and filled with a tantalizing layer of Nutella.

4 eggs, separated	
4 cups boiling water	**.9 L**
¾ cup sugar	**180 ml**
2 teaspoons grated lemon rind	**10 ml**
½ cup flour	**120 ml**
½ tablespoon cake yeast	**7 ml**
4 tablespoons vegetable sugar	**60 ml**
Nutella	
Powdered sugar	

- Whisk egg yolks with water. Add ½ cup (120 ml) sugar, lemon rind and a little salt and mix until creamy and smooth.
- Whisk egg whites in separate bowl. Add flour and remaining sugar. Mix in cake yeast.
- Slowly stir all ingredients and gradually add oil.
- Preheat oven to 375° (190° C).
- Grease and flour oven-safe dish. Pour mixture into dish and cook for 30 to 40 minutes. Remove from oven and cool completely.
- Slice cake in half horizontally. Spread thick layer of Nutella over bottom piece of cake. Place top back on and sprinkle with powdered sugar.

Serves 4 to 6.

Nutella is a hazelnut, chocolate spread found in most grocery stores next to the peanut butter.

Mele e Banane Fritte
(Fried Apples and Bananas)

This recipe is traditionally a Christmas Eve specialty served with a traditional dinner. Because it's is such a special treat, our family looks forward to eating it any time of the year.

2 medium apples, peeled, sliced	
2 bananas, peeled, sliced	
1 cup flour	**240 ml**
½ cup sparkling mineral water	**120 ml**
Powdered sugar	

- Heat cooking oil in large, deep skillet over medium heat and cover.
- Wash apples, peel and cut into ¼-inch (.6 cm) thick slices. Peel bananas and cut lengthwise into ¼-inch (.6 cm) thick slices. Set aside.
- Mix flour and sparkling mineral water in medium bowl. Stir and add dash of salt. (Batter should stick to fork without completely running off. If batter is too runny, add a little bit of flour. If batter is too thick, add a little more water.)
- Dip fruit into batter and completely coat. Carefully place fruit into hot oil and cook on all sides until light brown.
- Remove with slotted spoon and drain on paper towels. Sprinkle fruit with powdered sugar and serve.

Serves 4 to 6.

Crepes alla Nutella
(Crepes Filled with Nutella)

We would have to rank this as our top dessert. It has become a real tradition when our family visits from Italy. We all gather around the kitchen table after a long, good meal and watch while Mamma prepares this mouth-watering dessert.

1 ½ cups milk	360 ml
1 cup all-purpose flour	240 ml
2 eggs	
2 tablespoons sugar	30 ml
1 tablespoon cooking oil	15 ml
Nutella	
½ cup butter	120 ml
6 tablespoons sugar	90 ml
¾ cup orange juice	180 ml
½ cup Grand Marnier	120 ml

- Combine milk, flour, eggs, sugar, oil and dash of salt in large bowl to make batter. Mix with whisk or rotary beater until mixture blends well.
- Heat lightly greased 10-inch (25 cm) skillet. Drop in about 3 tablespoons (45 ml) batter, lift and tilt skillet to spread.
- Lightly brown on one side and flip to other side to brown. Remove and set aside. Repeat process until all batter is gone.
- Spread Nutella evenly on each crepe. Fold in half, then in half again to make a triangle shape.
- Combine butter and sugar in skillet and cook until sugar caramelizes. Add orange juice and bring to gentle boil.
- Add crepes and gently simmer for 2 minutes. Remove and set aside. Add Grand Marnier, bring to medium boil and stir continuously for 5 minutes. Liquid should be slightly thick.
- Place crepes on individual serving dishes. Pour desired amount of sauce and serve.

Makes 10 to 12 crepes.

Affogato
(Espresso Float)

Don't let this easy dessert fool you. It packs a powerful punch. Affogato means "drowned" in Italian and that is exactly what happens to the vanilla ice cream. A generous scoop of vanilla ice cream drowns in 1 or 2 shots of espresso topped with a dollop of whipped cream.

4 cups hot Italian espresso coffee, divided	**.9 L**
8 scoops vanilla ice cream	
4 tablespoons brandy, optional	**60 ml**
Whipped cream	

- In 4 individual serving bowls, place 2 scoops of vanilla ice cream.
- Pour 1 cup (240 ml) hot espresso coffee, 1 tablespoon (15 ml) brandy and a dollop of whipped cream to garnish. Serve and enjoy.

Serves 4.

Zabaglione
(Italian Eggnog Custard)

Zabaglione is classic Italian custard flavored with sweet wine and served warm or cold. It is often served over a slice of Ciambellone or fresh fruit such as fragole (strawberries) or pesche (peaches).

4 egg yolks	
4 tablespoons sugar	**60 ml**
4 tablespoons marsala wine	**60 ml**
Pinch of orange zest	

- Fill bottom half of double boiler with enough water so that top pan does not touch water (otherwise, custard will become lumpy when cooked.) Place on stove and simmer.
- Combine egg yolks, sugar and marsala wine in top saucepan. Whisk until ingredients blend well and texture is smooth.
- Place top pan in bottom pan of simmering water. Continue whisking until custard is light and foamy, about 7 minutes. Stir in orange zest and serve immediately.

Serves 4.

Torta al Rum e Noci
(Rum and Nut Cake)

3 egg yolks	
1 cup sugar, divided	240 ml
2½ cups flour, divided	600 ml
2 cups milk	480 ml
½ cup grated lemon peel	120 ml
1 cup butter softened	240 ml
4 eggs	
¾ cup sour cream	180 ml
1 teaspoon vanilla extract	5 ml
½ teaspoon nutmeg	2 ml
¼ teaspoon baking soda	1 ml
½ cup nuts, chopped	120 ml
½ cup dark rum	120 ml

- Preheat oven to 350° (176° C). Beat yolks and ¼ cup (60 ml) sugar in small mixing bowl. Slowly add ¼ cup (60 ml) flour. In small pot, bring milk just to brink of boiling. Remove from heat and pour over yolk mixture.

- Pour yolk mixture with milk back into pot. Place over medium heat, stir constantly and cook until mixture thickens. Remove from heat, add lemon peel and mix thoroughly. Place mixture in plastic container, cover and place in refrigerator to chill.

- Use mixer with paddle to cream butter and remaining sugar at high speed. Add eggs one at a time and make sure each one absorbs before adding another. Add sour cream and mix thoroughly. Add vanilla, nutmeg, baking soda and ¼ teaspoon (1 ml) salt. Decrease to medium speed, add remaining flour and mix for 1 minute. Gently fold in nuts until completely incorporated.

- Place batter into 1-quart (1 L) round or rectangular cake pan, leaving ½-inch (1.2 cm) space at the top. Place on the middle rack of oven for 50 to 60 minutes. Cake is done when surface cracks and toothpick inserted in center comes out clean.

- Remove cake from oven and cook for 15 minutes before removing from pan. When cake is completely cool, slice into 6 layers. On each layer, sprinkle some of rum and spread some of custard mixture. Finish by spreading remaining custard over entire surface of cake. Serve and enjoy!

Ricette Base

Basic Recipes

Sugo di Pomodoro Semplice
(Basic Red Sauce)

2 (28 ounce) cans whole peeled or crushed tomatoes	2 (796 g)
3 tablespoons olive oil	45 ml
2 garlic cloves, peeled, minced	
1 teaspoon crushed red pepper	5 ml
4 leaves fresh basil	

- Blend tomatoes until smooth. Add olive oil and garlic in large pot. Sauté garlic until just about golden.
- Add tomatoes, 2 teaspoons salt (10 ml), crushed red pepper and basil leaves. Reduce heat to low and simmer about 1½ hours.

Serves 4.

Besciamella
(Basic Bechamel Sauce)

½ cup (1 stick) butter	120 ml
4 tablespoons flour	60 ml
½ cup milk	120 ml
Dash of nutmeg	

- Melt butter in saucepan, gradually add flour and stir.
- Slowly pour in milk and continue to stir. Do not stop stirring or besciamella will be lumpy.
- Add dash of salt, pepper and nutmeg.

Ragú
(Basic Meat Sauce)

2 (28 ounce) cans whole peeled or crushed tomatoes	2 (796 g)
¼ cup finely chopped onion	60 ml
3 baby carrots, finely chopped	
½ rib celery, finely chopped	
3 tablespoons olive oil	45 ml
1 pound lean ground beef or ground turkey	.5 kg
⅓ cup white wine	80 ml
1 teaspoon dried oregano	5 ml
1 cube beef or vegetable bouillon, optional	

- Blend tomatoes until smooth. Chop onion, carrots, and celery as small as possible. (In Italy this process is called "battuto".)
- Add olive oil and "battuto" in large pot. Sauté until onions are translucent.
- Add ground beef and cook until brown. Add white wine, 2 teaspoons (10 ml) salt, 1 teaspoon pepper (5 ml) and oregano. Add beef or vegetable bouillon, if desired.
- Allow wine to cook out. Add blended tomatoes, reduce heat to low and simmer about 2 hours.

Pastella
(Batter for Vegetables)

1 **egg, beaten**	
1 **cup flour**	**240 ml**
½ **cup beer or sparkling mineral water**	**120 ml**

- Combine eggs, flour, beer or sparkling mineral water, a little salt and pepper to taste in separate bowl. Mix until all blend well.

Pastella
(Batter for Fruit)

1 **cup flour**	**240 ml**
½ **cup sparkling mineral water**	**120 ml**
Pinch of salt	

- Combine all ingredients in pan and mix well.

Brodo di Pollo
(Chicken Stock)

3 **tablespoons olive oil**	**45 ml**
½ **onion, whole**	
1 **rib celery, halved**	
6 **baby carrots, whole**	
½ **cut chicken**	
1 **cube vegetable bouillon**	

- Fill large pot with 10 cups (2.5 L) water and bring to boil. Add all ingredients, cover, reduce heat and simmer for 45 minutes or until chicken cooks thoroughly. Add salt and pepper to taste. Remove chicken and vegetables and set aside.

The Italian Family Cookbook
Recipe Names & Categories

To Order: *The Italian Family Cookbook*

Please send_____ hardcover copies @ $16.95 (U.S.) each $ _____

Texas residents add sales tax @ $1.40 each $ _____

Plus postage/handling @ $6.00 (1st copy) $ _____

$1.00 (each additional copy) $ _____

Check or Credit Card (Canada-credit card only)   **Total** $ _____

Charge to:

_____ MasterCard   _____ Visa

Account # _____

Expiration Date _____

Signature _____

Mail or Call:

Cookbook Resources
541 Doubletree Drive
Highland Village, Texas 75077
Toll Free (866) 229-2665
Fax (972) 317-6404

Name _____

Address _____

City _____ State _____ Zip _____

Telephone (Day)_____ (Evening) _____

— —

To Order: *The Italian Family Cookbook*

Please send_____ hardcover copies @ $16.95 (U.S.) each $ _____

Texas residents add sales tax @ $1.40 each $ _____

Plus postage/handling @ $6.00 (1st copy) $ _____

$1.00 (each additional copy) $ _____

Check or Credit Card (Canada-credit card only)   **Total** $ _____

Charge to:

_____ MasterCard   _____ Visa

Account # _____

Expiration Date _____

Signature _____

Mail or Call:

Cookbook Resources
541 Doubletree Drive
Highland Village, Texas 75077
Toll Free (866) 229-2665
Fax (972) 317-6404

Name _____

Address _____

City _____ State _____ Zip _____

Telephone (Day)_____ (Evening) _____

COOKBOOKS PUBLISHED BY COOKBOOK RESOURCES, LLC

The Ultimate Cooking with 4 Ingredients

Easy Cooking with 5 Ingredients

The Best of Cooking with 3 Ingredients

Gourmet Cooking with 5 Ingredients

Healthy Cooking with 4 Ingredients

Diabetic Cooking with 4 Ingredients

4-Ingredient Recipes for 30-Minute Meals

Essential 3-4-5 Ingredient Recipes

The Best 1001 Short, Easy Recipes

Easy Slow-Cooker Cookbook

Easy 1-Dish Meals

Essential Slow-Cooker Cooking

Quick Fixes with Cake Mixes

Casseroles to the Rescue

I Ain't On No Diet Cookbook

Kitchen Keepsakes/More Kitchen Keepsakes

Old-Fashioned Cookies

Grandmother's Cookies

Mother's Recipes

Recipe Keeper

Cookie Dough Secrets

Gifts for the Cookie Jar

All New Gifts for the Cookie Jar

Gifts in a Pickle Jar

Muffins In A Jar

Brownies In A Jar

Cookie Jar Magic

Easy Desserts

Bake Sale Bestsellers

The Bake Sale Cookbook

Quilters' Cooking Companion

Miss Sadie's Southern Cooking

Classic Tex-Mex and Texas Cooking

Classic Southwest Cooking

The Great Canadian Cookbook

The Best of Lone Star Legacy Cookbook

Cookbook 25 Years

Texas Longhorn Cookbook

Trophy Hunters' Wild Game Cookbook

Holiday Recipes

Little Taste of Texas

Little Taste of Texas II

Texas Peppers

Southwest Sizzler

Southwest Olé

Class Treats

Leaving Home

cookbook resources LLC
Bringing Families To The Table